How to Cope

The Welcoming Approach to Life's Challenges

Dr Claire Hayes

Gill & Macmillan

Gill & Macmillan
Hume Avenue, Park West, Dublin 12
www.gillmacmillanbooks.ie

© Dr Claire Hayes 2015
978 07171 6823 1

Typography design by Make Communication
Print origination by Carole Lynch
Printed and bound by CPI Group (UK) Ltd, CR0 4YY

This book is typeset in Linotype Minion and Neue Helvetica.

The paper used in this book comes from the wood pulp
of managed forests. For every tree felled, at least one tree
is planted, thereby renewing natural resources.

A CIP catalogue record for this book is available
from the British Library.

5 4 3 2 1

About the author

Dr Claire Hayes has worked in a variety of roles over the past thirty years, including principal teacher, clinical psychologist, lecturer, educational psychologist, executive coach, researcher and clinical director. The focus of her work continues to be on how best to help people cope with whatever is causing them distress. She has developed a particular format known as the 'Coping Triangle' to teach the basic principles of cognitive behavioural therapy (CBT) as a way of helping people understand the nature of their distress and take practical steps to do something to improve things. Her first book, *Stress Relief for Teachers: The Coping Triangle*, was published in 2006.

Dr Hayes's work with individuals and organisations has evolved from 'coping with life's challenges' to welcoming them as opportunities to learn, grow and respond proactively. She currently works as a Consultant Clinical Psychologist (www.drclairehayes.ie) and as Clinical Director with Aware (www.aware.ie).

Feedback from people who have benefited from Claire Hayes's unique way of working:

'Claire provided me with techniques to help me calm myself when I was thinking about something that I knew would upset me.'

—EMMA, AGED 32

'I had suffered from anxiety and panic periodically since my early twenties. I was at a particularly low ebb when my doctor gave me Claire's number. Without exaggeration, she changed my life. I found the Cognitive Behavioural Therapy particularly effective and also the Coping Triangle. Claire gave me the tools to manage my anxiety and panic. I also found Claire's gentle, calm, non-judgemental manner helped me accept that I wasn't alone.'

—'MARY', AGED 52

'When I went to see Claire, I was lost. To put it simply she gave me direction, she gave me a sense of purpose, and a sense of hope. Only recently I feel I have started to take control of my own life again and I feel that I am worth something. It has been a very difficult journey, but today I feel that I have got stronger.'

—ENDA, AGED 35

In memory of Noreen Barrett,
my aunt and friend.

The Guest House

This being human is a guest house.
Every morning a new arrival.

A joy, a depression, a meanness,
Some momentary awareness comes
As an unexpected visitor.

Welcome and entertain them all!
Even if they're a crowd of sorrows,
who violently sweep your house
empty of its furniture,
still treat each guest honourably.
He may be clearing you out
for some new delight.

The dark thought, the shame, the malice,
meet them at the door laughing,
and invite them in.

Be grateful for whoever comes,
because each has been sent
as a guide from beyond.

—MEWLANA JALALUDDIN RUMI (TRANSLATED BY
COLEMAN BARKS), FROM *THE ESSENTIAL RUMI.*

Contents

Acknowledgements

Sometimes when my father Liam completed a task he would take a few moments to sit in quiet appreciation. He was very wise and is greatly missed. As I reflect on how this book has come to be, I too sit in appreciation and am aware of the following people whom I would like to acknowledge and thank:

- The many people who have trusted me to work with them and who have taught me about human strength, courage and resilience in coping with adversity
- My mother, Joy, who is now even more precious
- Aisling, Brian and Paul and my extended family
- Aoife McKiernan, Anne O'Shea, the teachers I have been so fortunate to have, particularly Professor Mark Morgan, and my friends: I am blessed that there are too many to mention by name
- My colleagues, particularly the volunteers and staff of Aware
- The staff of Gill & Macmillan, particularly Deirdre Nolan, who welcomed this book and who has been so supportive throughout, and also Deirdre Rennison Kunz, Teresa Daly and Deborah Marsh
- James

Míle buíochas—a thousand thanks!

Part 1

The 'Welcoming Approach'

Introduction

And suddenly you know: it's time to start
something new and trust the magic of beginnings.
—MEISTER ECKHART

How many of us can honestly say that we welcome every challenge that life brings? While some challenges can be exciting and can stretch us to discover abilities and strengths we never knew we had, others may be very difficult. At any moment we can hear news that causes us to think thoughts such as 'This is terrible,' 'How am I ever going to cope?' 'This is all my fault,' 'I didn't do enough,' or even 'This is too much—I can't take any more.'

Thoughts like these can cause us to feel upset, anxious, sad, angry, guilty, embarrassed, ashamed or depressed. Life's challenges vary and, interestingly, something that may seem overwhelming for one person can be exhilarating for someone else.

Some people are naturally good at coping and tend not to get too distressed by anything. They tend to be flexible and adaptable and are skilled at asking for, and taking, help. Many of us, though, struggle at asking for help, seeing it as a weakness to do so. If we have a lot to deal with already and don't realise how much of a struggle it is to manage, it may take only a very small challenge to cause us incredible distress. Challenges that we could easily cope with one day might be just too much on a different day. We may react by withdrawing, lashing out, or even harming ourselves or someone else. It can be a relief to remember that we always have choices about how we react to life's challenges.

This book is a book of hope. While life itself teaches us that life can be challenging, this book invites you to welcome these challenges and the feelings and thoughts that you have about them, so that you are better able to deal with them proactively. It does so by describing the 'Welcoming Approach' and illustrating, through a number of case studies, how it can be used to help people develop resilience and strength.

It's important to emphasise that I have devised each of these case studies specifically for this book. While the people I describe are all fictitious, their challenges are similar to those facing real people whom I have been privileged to work with over the past twenty years as a clinical psychologist and an educational psychologist.

Some of the challenges are universal, while others are very specific. In creating one particular story about a young man who had a heart transplant I was inspired by the courage, dignity and resilience of my friend Aoife, who underwent a double lung transplant in 2013. She has given me her permission to acknowledge her strength in coping with one of life's greatest challenges.

In writing about the 'Welcoming Approach' I have also drawn on a range of learning experiences I have had the opportunity to experience over the past thirty years.

———

This book is in two parts. The first describes the Welcoming Approach in detail. It presents two case studies to illustrate how our thoughts, beliefs and actions can affect our feelings. Part 2 deals with how the Welcoming Approach can be applied to helping us with particular challenges that we will all face at some stage in our lives: pressure, rejection, loss, failure, success and change. These are not our only life challenges and may not be our greatest. Life is very much an individual experience, and some of the stories you read in this book may not be relevant to you at this time. If that is so I invite you to welcome your feelings, pay attention to your thoughts, question what you believe, and concentrate on what helpful actions you can take.

I hope you will enjoy reading this book and will find it informative. Sometimes looking at life's challenges can actually result in our feeling pressured and overwhelmed, particularly if we think there is nothing we can do to change things. If that happens to you, please welcome your feelings as indicators that you may need some support at this time, and follow up by talking to someone who cares about you and who is in a position to provide real support. This may be a family member, a friend, or a GP. As you will see, feelings generally make sense, but we don't need to panic because we have them: we just need to do something about them!

Chapter 1
Welcome to the Welcoming Approach

Céad míle fáilte: A hundred thousand welcomes

Picture a three-year-old child playing. She is holding a balloon and is laughing as it bounces in front of her. Suddenly it breaks free of her grip. She stands puzzled for a moment before beginning to cry. Most of us would do our best to rush to the rescue, jump to catch the balloon, anticipating her grateful smile. Sometimes that may happen; often, though, the balloon ascends quickly out of reach and bursts on the branch of a tree.

It can be very difficult to listen to the cries of the little girl. Many of us would wish at that moment that we had a bigger, brighter, better balloon to give her so as to take her mind off her loss and make her feel happy once more. Few of us would use that moment to explain to her that the rest of her life will be just like this. When she has something precious that she thinks makes her feel happy it can blow away, without any warning, and burst. As we cannot get the original balloon back, some of us might comfort the child and tell her not to worry and that we will buy her an even better balloon. Some of us might scold her for crying, tell her that it was her own fault anyway for not holding on tightly enough, and hope that she will have learnt her lesson for the future.

Will we allow that little girl to express her feelings of upset and anger, or will we teach her to smile and pretend that 'it doesn't really matter,' to make us feel better? Our response as adults will depend on our own understanding of the loss of the balloon for the child, on our own experiences of loss and on our own comfortableness with feelings.

Picture the little girl—let's call her Anna—going home believing that pain follows joy and that loss follows laughter. As Anna gets older she may become one of the increasing number of people who experience anxiety or depression. She may cling to people or to objects and find change in her life very difficult to cope with. She may develop a more hopeless outlook on life and find it difficult to have anything of beauty or value. 'What's the point?' she may ask, without expecting an answer. 'Life is only going to destroy it anyway.'

This story can have a different ending. While we may wish to protect Anna from the pain and distress of losing her balloon, our protection might not help her to develop coping skills. Instead we can use the bursting balloon as an opportunity for her to develop resilience and to learn that she is able to cope with upsetting things.

Now think about Richard, one of Anna's classmates. When he was three years old he fell and hurt his knee, his dog died, and his sister accidentally stood on his favourite toy. Each time something upsetting happened he burst into tears and his mother immediately picked him up and cuddled him. Richard wasn't able to name his predominant feeling as 'shame' as he listened to his father shouting at his mother to stop treating him like a pathetic baby. He had no way of knowing that his father was reacting in this way as a result of his own experiences of being beaten for crying when he was a child. All Richard knew was that it was not all right for him to cry, that he was weak, not strong like his father and not good enough. This led him to cry even more, and while he craved his mother's comfort he also resented her for treating him like a baby and alienating him from his father.

Richard could not have explained how he felt when he was three years old, when he was thirteen or even when he was thirty. His feeling of confusion grew as he grew older. His uncertainty about when, or even if, it was all right to express feelings grew too. He discovered alcohol when he was fourteen and saw how all his self-doubts and anxieties just disappeared. He didn't like the look of pain in his mother's eyes when she realised that he was drinking heavily, though he craved the look of respect he thought he saw in his father's eyes. Would we be surprised to know that Richard's first and second marriages failed, that his children were afraid of him, and that he became more deeply unhappy as he grew older?

What's going on? How is it that, despite an increasing awareness of the importance of the early childhood years, of education, of libraries of self-help books and a range of evidence-based therapies, including cognitive behavioural therapy (CBT) and mindfulness-based therapies, the World Health Organisation predicts that by 2030 depression will be the principal global burden of disease, surpassing heart disease and cancer? Could it be that the rate of depression, anxiety, eating disorders, substance abuse and unhappiness is increasing in the world because we strive to feel happy and are not able to cope with not feeling happy?

• The Welcoming Approach invites us to welcome our feelings of distress as we would welcome a precious child. It is beautiful to hold a baby who has just been bathed and is wrapped in a warm blanket; it is not so beautiful to have the same baby be sick all over us. We accept, though, that this is what babies do, and we don't expect them to be all smiles all the time. Our tolerance for cries diminishes as the child gets older.

When we drive a car and a warning light flashes, most of us make arrangements to get the car examined. We heed the warning and we take action. How might life have been for

Richard if he had learnt this at a young age? How would the world be if each of us learnt to see our feelings as warnings, to welcome them as warnings and to act on the warnings?

When people are feeling low, upset, angry, anxious or sad, the last thing they might want to do is to welcome those feelings into their lives and into their hearts. Instead they may well do their very best to get rid of them. They may take medication, talk to friends or therapists, eat or drink to excess or perhaps even deny the feelings altogether. The feelings will not go away, however: they will stay there until they are recognised and responded to.

My work as a clinical psychologist involves helping people to recognise and be gentle with these uncomfortable feelings and— to quote the late Susan Jeffers—'do it anyway.' The natural instinct for any of us is to avoid something that makes us feel bad. The snag is that by avoiding it we give power to the object itself, as well as to the thoughts that cause us to feel bad. So where does 'welcoming' come in?

A few years ago I received an unexpected bill. I was not prepared for the intensity of the feelings of shame, upset and embarrassment I experienced and wondered why my reaction was so extreme. Deciding to 'practise what I preach,' I read some of the books I recommend to other people. One of them contained an exercise in which I was to deliberately focus on experiences I had had in the past that made me feel good. As I began to think about this I had memories of many experiences of myself as a child, a teenager and a young woman being welcomed by my parents, my aunts, my grandmothers and my friends. My Aunty Noreen used to say that as a child I brought my own welcome with me and would arrive running towards her with my arms open, ready for the big hug I was expecting. When I reflected on my bill I realised that I could welcome my feelings of distress as a wake-up call for me to be more

organised. The more I began to welcome them as an invitation
for me to act, the easier it was for me to do something proactive. Then, over time, I did feel better.

Since then I have used the Welcoming Approach with clients
who have experienced a wide range of distressing feelings,
including anger, anxiety, fear, guilt and shame. This approach
uses the 'Coping Triangle', which is my way of explaining the
basic principles of cognitive behavioural therapy to help people
understand how they are feeling, to become aware of their
thoughts and beliefs and to focus particularly on how they can
act in a helpful way to improve the quality of their lives.
Towards the end of the book we will come back to Anna's and
Richard's stories and see how the Welcoming Approach might
help them.

So what is the Welcoming Approach? It involves recognising,
accepting and then welcoming feelings as messengers so that we
can act proactively to improve our situation. It also involves
welcoming the ability we all have to recognise our thoughts and
actions as 'helpful' or 'unhelpful' and how we can then focus on
acting in a helpful way. Through this process we become aware
of what we believe about ourselves, our lives and our future.

Ultimately, the Welcoming Approach is a gentle and powerful way for us to turn feelings of distress into helpful action.

You may have noticed that I use questions a lot. I do this
deliberately. When I was a child, some of my teachers didn't
like me asking 'stupid questions'. I only learnt gradually that
there is no such thing as a stupid question. If we think about
what we want to know, we are more likely to find out the
answers. Here are some questions for you to ask yourself so
that you can maximise your learning from this book.

What does the word 'welcome' mean to you? Now picture
yourself arriving at someone's house and receiving a warm
welcome. What was it that made you feel welcome? Was it the

tone of voice of the person? Was it a hug? Was it that you were immediately offered a cup of tea?

Think about the person you enjoy welcoming most. Why? What is it about him or her that makes it easy for you to be welcoming? How do you demonstrate your welcome? Now take a few moments to read slowly Derek Walcott's wonderful poem 'Love After Love.'

The time will come
when, with elation,
you will greet yourself arriving
at your own door, in your own mirror
and each will smile at the other's welcome,
and say, sit here. Eat.
You will love again the stranger who was your self.
Give wine. Give bread. Give back your heart
to itself, to the stranger who has loved you
all your life, whom you ignored
for another, who knows you by heart.
Take down the love letters from the bookshelf,
the photographs, the desperate notes,
peel your own image from the mirror.
Sit. Feast on your life.

Had you any reaction to this poem as you read it? I had. I had a very strong reaction that took me completely by surprise the first time I read it. I pictured myself hearing my doorbell ring and walking to the door to open it, only to discover with an acute sense of disappointment that it was 'only me.' Instead of welcoming myself in I could hear myself muttering, 'Oh, it's you,' and walking back into the house, leaving myself to follow or not. How could I have expected other people to like ◑ me, value me, appreciate me and love me if I didn't see myself as someone I would welcome to my home? I thought a lot about that.

How might life be for each of us if we opened our doors, our lives and our hearts to feelings of distress; if, rather than blaming ourselves for not being 'good enough,' we gently acknowledge that this is a difficult time for us and that we need to take care of ourselves and do something proactive to help us feel better?

This book is a guide for you in doing just that. It gently helps you to become aware of how your feelings, thoughts, beliefs and actions can interact and encourages you to be proactive in how you cope with life's challenges. These ideas have evolved from developments in psychology called cognitive behavioural therapy (CBT), acceptance commitment therapy (ACT) and mindfulness. Some of the ideas that form the basis of this book are:

- Feelings are messengers.
- While feelings can be very distressful they are in themselves neither 'good' nor 'bad'.
- If feelings make sense, they are all right.
- Our responses can be helpful or unhelpful, depending on our thoughts, beliefs and actions.
- We can all learn from challenging situations.
- We can all learn to cope.

The core of the Welcoming Approach can be described in one sentence: 'Let's welcome our feelings of distress as messengers, listen to what they are telling us, and respond proactively!'

Chapter 2
Who cares how you feel?

This being human is a guest house.
Every morning a new arrival.

A joy, a depression, a meanness,
Some momentary awareness comes
As an unexpected visitor.

—MEWLANA JALALUDDIN RUMI

Right now, how do you feel? Now ask yourself, Who cares how you feel? Do you? Does anyone else? The phrase 'Who cares?' can imply that no-one does. That may be true, but maybe it is not true.

Sometimes people can care too much about how they feel and unwittingly facilitate themselves in feeling worse. They may care too much about how we feel too. They frequently ask, 'How do you feel?' with a genuine regard for our well-being. They want us to feel better, and if we were to ask them why, they would probably say that they don't like to see us unhappy. Automatically, we may assume that that is very kind of them and appreciate how caring they are towards us. We may not realise how their concern could be keeping us focused on how we are feeling, with at times very serious consequences.

Imagine that you have been experiencing severe heart problems and have been on the waiting-list for a heart transplant for six months. You know that time is running out and that if you don't receive a donor heart soon you will probably die. If someone was to ask you, 'How do you feel?' you might respond that you feel anxious, upset, worried or hopeful. It would be easy to see how feelings such as these would make absolute sense. Few people would expect you to feel elated if you were in such a position.

Now imagine that you have received a heart transplant, surgery has been successful and the medical team is feeling relieved and delighted. Your family is probably feeling relieved and delighted too. Their feelings of relief and delight would make a lot of sense: indeed we would be dismayed if someone said that they felt disappointed and angry that you now had a better chance of living a longer and healthier life.

How do you think you might feel a few days after your surgery? Wonderful? Probably not. It's likely that you might feel sore, upset, confused, worried, frightened and maybe even guilty. These feelings, in my view, would make just as much sense as the feeling of relief and delight from the medical team and your family and friends. The feelings of pain are easy to understand, but people who care about you might feel distressed that you are not experiencing feelings of relief and delight too. They may not understand that you are feeling guilty because you got a heart that you think other people waiting would have deserved more than you, and sad because you are thinking of the person who died.

If you tell them what you are thinking you can be almost guaranteed that they will concentrate their energies on telling you why you should not feel guilty or sad. Their reassurance will not work, though. If you then confide that you feel anxious as you worry about possible rejection, they most probably will once again spend time reassuring you that the doctors are wonderful, the medication is wonderful, and you are not to think about anything going wrong.

Do you think their attempts to reassure you would make you feel better? I think not. Reassurance does not work, because your body could reject your new heart, and you know that.

Let's fast-forward a month. By now some of the physical pain is easing. Everyone is asking you if you're feeling better. You're not—in fact you're becoming increasingly distressed, because you actually feel worse. You feel more upset, more frightened and more anxious. The more people ask you how you're feeling the more you focus on how you are feeling and the more you worry because you don't feel better. You wonder if you will ever feel better again and feel even more distressed. Why on earth would you welcome those feelings of fear and upset? My suggestion is because these feelings make sense. They make sense because of what is happening in your life and because of your thoughts, actions and beliefs about what is happening in your life.

STEPHEN

It might be difficult to think of yourself having a heart transplant, so let's switch to imagining that your friend Stephen has just had this surgery. You're feeling frustrated and upset as, despite all your encouragement and reassurance, he says he is feeling worse and worse.

Let's look at what Stephen is actually thinking and what he's doing, using an inverted triangle. This is the first of three steps of what I call the Coping Triangle. It is the key tool in the Welcoming Approach and is my way of explaining the basic principles of cognitive behavioural therapy to help people understand and respond to their feelings of distress. Fig. 2.1 shows Stephen's thoughts, feelings and actions four weeks after his surgery.

Stephen may feel some relief as he writes down his thoughts, his feelings and his actions. The process of doing this exercise may cause him to think, 'What's the point in doing this? This is stupid. Nothing is going to help me.' He will probably then feel even worse. As he notices that he feels worse he may then worry about himself even more.

Fig. 2.1: Step 1 of Stephen's Coping Triangle

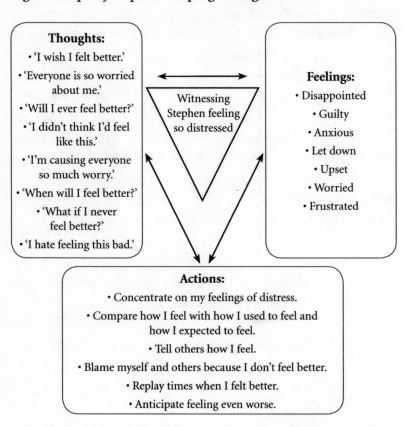

Thoughts:
- 'I wish I felt better.'
- 'Everyone is so worried about me.'
- 'Will I ever feel better?'
- 'I didn't think I'd feel like this.'
- 'I'm causing everyone so much worry.'
- 'When will I feel better?'
- 'What if I never feel better?'
- 'I hate feeling this bad.'

Witnessing Stephen feeling so distressed

Feelings:
- Disappointed
- Guilty
- Anxious
- Let down
- Upset
- Worried
- Frustrated

Actions:
- Concentrate on my feelings of distress.
- Compare how I feel with how I used to feel and how I expected to feel.
- Tell others how I feel.
- Blame myself and others because I don't feel better.
- Replay times when I felt better.
- Anticipate feeling even worse.

Let's see how doing step 1 of the Coping Triangle makes you feel. Imagine that you are someone who cares deeply about Stephen, and now complete the thoughts, feelings and actions in fig. 2.2.

Fig. 2.2: Step 1 of my Coping Triangle

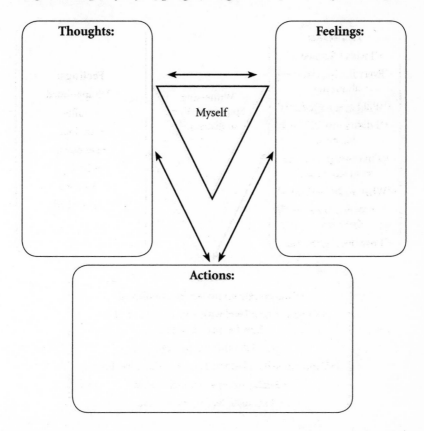

Now let's assume that I am someone who cares deeply about Stephen and I have just completed the first step of the Coping Triangle, as illustrated in fig. 2.3.

Fig. 2.3: Step 2 of Claire's Coping Triangle

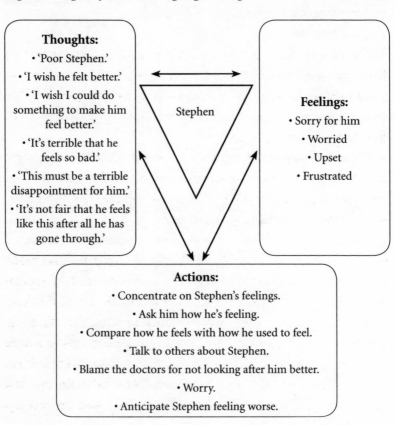

Thoughts:
- 'Poor Stephen.'
- 'I wish he felt better.'
- 'I wish I could do something to make him feel better.'
- 'It's terrible that he feels so bad.'
- 'This must be a terrible disappointment for him.'
- 'It's not fair that he feels like this after all he has gone through.'

Stephen

Feelings:
- Sorry for him
- Worried
- Upset
- Frustrated

Actions:
- Concentrate on Stephen's feelings.
- Ask him how he's feeling.
- Compare how he feels with how he used to feel.
- Talk to others about Stephen.
- Blame the doctors for not looking after him better.
- Worry.
- Anticipate Stephen feeling worse.

So how do you feel now having done that exercise? Were any of my thoughts, feelings or actions similar to yours? Do you feel discouraged and perhaps overwhelmed now, or do you feel interested? There's an underlying assumption in this situation that there's something wrong with how Stephen is feeling and an automatic urgency to 'fix him' to make him feel better.

Step 2 of the Coping Triangle involves asking the following four questions:

1. Do my feelings make sense?
2. Are my thoughts 'helpful' or 'unhelpful'?

3. What do I believe?

4. Are my actions 'helpful' or 'unhelpful'?

The first question is to ask whether our feelings make sense. Do they? Do Stephen's feelings make sense? I know that we would all like him to feel better, as it is distressing and hard for him, as well as for us, to feel so much pain, upset and anxiety. But do his feelings make sense?

When we step back a little we can see that they do. How could we expect Stephen to feel any differently when we first consider that he has had a heart transplant and, secondly, realise what he is thinking and doing?

Do our feelings make sense? Mine do; and even though I don't know how you feel I'm guessing that your feelings make sense too! It would seem bizarre if I cared so much for Stephen and at the same felt delighted that he was obviously in distress.

My feelings also make sense because of what I'm thinking, what I'm doing and what I believe. I will explain this in a little while when we look at the remaining three questions that form step 2 of the Coping Triangle; for now let's stay with the first question, 'Do Stephen's feelings, your feelings and my feelings make sense?'

I see people as volcanoes, with feelings instead of lava. When we are young children we learn that it is great and acceptable to feel happy and good. We learn that it doesn't feel nice to feel angry, upset, guilty, ashamed, disappointed, hurt or anxious. We also learn that other people do not like us to experience these feelings either and do their best to help us 'feel better' and 'be happy.' Why? I think the main reason is that few of us are actually comfortable with our own feelings of distress and can be even more uncomfortable with those of other people. Pretending that we feel good when we don't tends not to work, as the pressure of those repressed feelings can build up and explode. This can be extremely frightening for the person who explodes as well as for the people who witness it.

Bottling up feelings may work for a while, but often they leak out in the form of sarcasm or passive-aggressive behaviour. Some people are really good at repressing their feelings, to the extent that they actually think they feel fine. Their body knows differently, though, and if those feelings are not expressed they can cause severe difficulties over time, such as depression, anxiety and perhaps other illnesses.

What would it be like if we used the Welcoming Approach instead of dismissing, blocking or worrying about our feelings? If Stephen was to welcome his feelings as messengers that make sense he would then be freed to consider the other three questions in step 2 of the Coping Triangle. When we stand back a little we can see that we all feel anxious and are worrying that Stephen may never feel better. Let's put some pin holes into the volcano, let steam out (which may even be in the form of tears) and have a closer look at anxiety, which I think is the key.

What is anxiety? Let's consider that one of our ancestors, thousands of years ago, was sent out from the tribe to hunt a bear. Picture him meeting an enormous bear, realising with horror that he could easily be killed, and instantly deciding to run to safety instead of staying to fight. His body's wonderful 'fight or flight' mechanism is instantly activated, triggering his body to produce adrenaline, which gives him the energy to run faster than he would ever have realised.

After a rest period he heads out into the wilderness again to successfully fight a bear. He then has a good rest, allowing his body to recover (fig. 2.4). Alternatively, he meets a huge bear and decides to run, using up some adrenaline. Then he finds another bear, decides that this is too big also, and runs again; then, seeing a third bear, he thinks he can fight, successfully kills it, using up his adrenaline, and then finally relaxes (fig. 2.5).

Contrast our ancestor's experience with ours. How often is our fight-or-flight mechanism activated every day? I see it working as easily as a light switch. If I turn on a switch, light comes on. If someone else turns on the switch, light comes on. If someone accidentally turns it on, light comes on. The light switch responds to being triggered, regardless of whether it is activated on purpose or by accident. Our fight-or-flight mechanism operates in a similar way. It is turned on by real things that cause danger, or by things that we think will cause us danger.

There are three essential differences between how we respond to stress and how our ancestors did. The first is that we are often not fully relaxed in the first place and may in fact be at quite a high level of stress most of the time, as illustrated in fig. 2.6 below. The second is that our fight-or-flight switch is more often triggered by thoughts of danger than by actual danger; and the third difference is that, unlike our ancestor, we don't generally allow our bodies to relax properly before reactivating our stress response.

Fig. 2.4: Our ancestor fights a bear and then relaxes

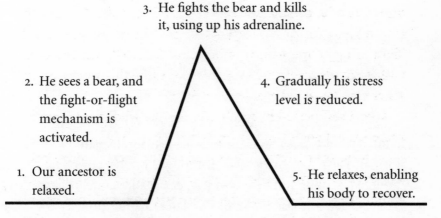

3. He fights the bear and kills it, using up his adrenaline.

2. He sees a bear, and the fight-or-flight mechanism is activated.

4. Gradually his stress level is reduced.

1. Our ancestor is relaxed.

5. He relaxes, enabling his body to recover.

Fig. 2.5: *Our ancestor runs, goes to fight, runs, fights, and then relaxes*

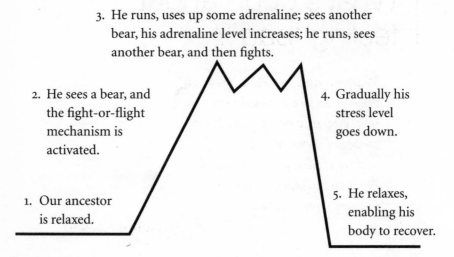

3. He runs, uses up some adrenaline; sees another bear, his adrenaline level increases; he runs, sees another bear, and then fights.

2. He sees a bear, and the fight-or-flight mechanism is activated.

4. Gradually his stress level goes down.

1. Our ancestor is relaxed.

5. He relaxes, enabling his body to recover.

Fig. 2.6: *We don't fight, we don't run: we stress*

2. Our fight-or-flight mechanism is activated by external events, and by our thoughts.

3. We don't relax but stay at a high level of arousal.

1. Unlike our ancestor, we are not relaxed to begin with!

The Welcoming Approach invites Stephen to see his feelings of anxiety and stress in relation to his heart transplant as being normal. He may not be aware, though, of the power of his thoughts, actions and beliefs to trigger his adrenaline response. We will look at these in detail in a later chapter; for now, let's turn to look at why it can actually be good to 'feel bad'!

Chapter 3
What's good about feeling 'bad'?

Welcome and entertain them all!
Even if they're a crowd of sorrows,
who violently sweep your house
empty of its furniture,
still treat each guest honourably.
He may be clearing you out
for some new delight.

—MEWLANA JALALUDDIN RUMI

The immediate answer to that question is 'Nothing.' Few of us like to feel 'bad', and even fewer like someone we love to feel bad. Think of the lengths we will go to in order to get someone to feel 'better'. Perhaps we have too little tolerance for feelings that some people describe as 'negative'. As we have seen with the story of Stephen, our reaction when someone tells us that they don't feel good is to immediately do our very best to cheer them up and make them feel good again. We do it instinctively, thinking that we're doing this because we care so much for the other person and want them to feel better. It may be a bit of a shock to realise that sometimes, perhaps many times, we do it because we don't like how we ourselves feel when we see someone else feeling distressed!

Before I began studying psychology I saw the job of a psychologist as helping people to feel better. I still thought this some years later when I was training to work as a clinical psychologist. The way it worked, I naïvely thought, was that people would realise they were not feeling happy, would come to me and tell me their stories and leave feeling better. I wonder when I began to realise that it just didn't work that way!

While some people do make an appointment with me because they don't feel happy and they want me to make them feel better, I now know that I don't have the power to do that. I don't think that anyone has. I can help people to become aware of how they feel, work with them to determine if their feelings make sense and suggest steps to take that might make them feel worse in the short term but over time will result in their feeling better.

It might seem puzzling to you that I suggest to people that they do something that may make them feel worse. One example of this might be when people feel anxious about going on a plane. They may have avoided plane journeys for some time, so even my suggestion that they go to an airport can cause feelings of anxiety. Rather than seeing this as proof that there is something wrong, I encourage them to welcome the feeling of anxiety as a sign that they are actually doing something to improve things. It is a paradox, really, and I often use the example that the treatment for cancer does not necessarily make someone feel good!

The Welcoming Approach provides a framework for people to welcome difficult feelings as an invitation to understand them and to do something about them. This might not be easy, as the story of a woman I have called Joanne illustrates. Like the other stories in this book, her issues are real, though she is not.

JOANNE

Joanne is a 34-year-old woman who describes herself as the mother of two children and as having a wonderful husband, three close friends and a part-time job that she loves. She doesn't understand why, when people tell her that she is so lucky, she immediately feels guilty. She doesn't feel lucky at all. She has two sons, but she doesn't have the daughter she has always dreamed of. She now dreads meeting her friends, as so much of their conversation revolves around the day-to-day tasks of mothering their daughters. Joanne feels too ashamed to tell them that she would love to have her make-up ruined by a pretty little daughter who loves dressing up in her mother's shoes. She has no idea how harshly she torments herself for 'disowning' her boys, and doesn't realise that she hides her true feelings by constantly repeating stories of how wonderful, absolutely wonderful, it is to be the mother of boys.

Joanne is afraid that if she got pregnant again and had a boy she would be so devastated that she would reject him. She lies awake at night haunted by how awful a person she is to treat a new little baby like that. It's as if she has already given birth to a third son and rejected him. She feels she is a fraud and worries that she is close to cracking up under the pressure. She has noticed that, despite her best attempts to smile and to constantly look as if she is in great form, her unhappiness is beginning to become obvious.

The tipping-point for her in seeking help was the look of sadness in her husband's eyes when she turned away from his attempt to kiss her when he came in from work. In that moment she saw her marriage beginning to end, her boys commuting between two different houses, her dealing badly with her husband's new wife and ultimately that she would live out the rest of her life as a sad, lonely, unhappy woman. She couldn't tell anyone that she felt like this, as she assumed they would all immediately tell her how wonderful her husband is (which she knows), how gorgeous her two sons are (which she knows) and how great a mother she is (which she does not and cannot believe). So, in desperation, she makes an appointment and comes to see me.

Let's follow Joanne's story as we enter my office together for her first visit. As she sits down she looks at me with tears in her eyes and asks me to please, please make this work. When I gently ask her how she would know whether or not this works she tells me that she will feel better and will be 'back to herself' and able to continue the rest of her life feeling happy. Twenty years ago I would have taken on the challenge and done my best to make her feel better so that she would leave my office feeling happy. I probably would have seen myself as having failed in my job if I didn't do that, and I would definitely have gone home berating myself for not being good enough if I noticed a look of sadness in her eyes as she left, thanking me for 'having tried anyway.'

I don't work like that any more. Instead I first explain a little bit about myself and how I work as well as the limits to confidentiality. I take some contact information and then work with Joanne to review crucial events in her life. This gives me an overview of her history and why she has chosen to come to me as well as helping us to examine together her patterns of strengths and vulnerabilities.

We all have difficulties and challenges, and how we cope with them can depend on a host of factors, including our age, gender, order in the family, relationship with our parents and siblings, personality, health, intellectual ability, quality of friendship, and occupation. Through such experiences we learn to develop our inner strength and resilience, or we learn to become more vulnerable to an inherent sense of ourselves as 'not being good enough.'

Here is a summary of Joanne's story. She is the eldest of three children. Her first brother was born when she was three years old and her second brother was born five years later. She described herself as always having had a good relationship with her brothers and looked surprised when I asked if she thought that being the eldest, and the only girl, had an effect on her. She immediately said no but then looked a little upset as she quietly explained that she always wanted to have a sister. She had asked once when she was about ten years old if she could have a sister and was so shocked by her mother's sharp response that she never asked again.

Joanne did not know until she was pregnant herself with her first child that her mother had had a miscarriage when she was twelve weeks pregnant, two years before her second son was born. Now, twenty-two years later, Joanne wondered if the embryo had been male or female. Fighting to hold back the tears, she then described how different she had felt in secondary school when her friends talked about borrowing clothes from their big sisters, or teaching their little sisters how to put on make-up. She had always felt that she was missing out, as her two brothers were so preoccupied with sport and their own friends that they didn't really see her as being part of their lives in the same way that her friends' sisters seemed to.

Joanne described herself as always having been in the top three academically throughout primary school, secondary school and university. She had close friends, and while she lost contact with some of them she is still close to one of them. She wasn't particularly pleased with how she did in her final exams in secondary school, explaining that she had been ill with pneumonia eight weeks before and that while she had recovered fully by the time of her first exam she had missed out on two months of revision. She didn't know what she wanted to do next and described herself as 'aimlessly doing an arts degree.' She was determined that she was not going to follow her mother into a career as a secondary teacher and instead chose to do a postgraduate course in business.

At that point Joanne met her future husband, Mike, and she explained with a slight smile that any notions she had of being a career woman disappeared overnight. Mike is a successful accountant, and financially there has been no need for Joanne to work outside the home. Her two boys are seven and five, and since her youngest son began school she helps out in her husband's office, doing part-time administrative work.

With a shrug Joanne described her brothers as living their own lives, one in England and one in America, and explained that they were both very good at keeping in contact with their parents. Both her mother and father are in good health, and Joanne visits them every week. She smiled as she said that her parents' neighbours tell them how lucky they are to have a daughter to look after them. Almost immediately she seemed startled by tears beginning to roll down her cheeks. She brushed them away crossly and looked as if she was pulling herself together. I could almost hear the thoughts in her head screaming at her to stop making a fool of herself, to stop being so dramatic and stop being so childish. My heart went out to her as I sat quietly waiting.

After a few moments Joanne smiled again and said, 'Well, that's why I'm here, really. I'm afraid I'm going mad. I just can't seem to convince myself that my life is wonderful as it is. I wake up in the morning long before Mike does and I promise myself that today will be different, today will be the day I really appreciate the life I have, and today will be the day I get on with things.'

She looked embarrassed as she explained how much she hates, really hates, the part of her that is jealous of her friends. She gave a half-hearted laugh as she told me that recently she watched a television programme in which women who wanted to have more than two children were described as selfish by women who were not able to have any. Why, she asked me, could she not be grateful for the wonderful sons she has, instead of longing for a little girl? With more tears running down her face she looked at me with a hint of desperation and said, 'Please make me feel better.'

Right now I invite you to take a few moments to check in with yourself and catch what you are thinking, how you are feeling and what you are doing as you read Joanne's story. Are you thinking, 'Oh, for goodness' sake, she's so wrapped up in herself she needs a good wake-up call!'? If you're thinking this I would expect that you're feeling annoyed and impatient. You may be thinking about women you know who also have two boys, or indeed you may have two sons yourself and may be comparing Joanne's reaction with theirs, or yours.

You may, on the other hand, be thinking something like 'That poor woman! Why is she so hard on herself? What is the huge crime she thinks she has committed by wanting to have a baby girl?' If so, you may feel compassionate and concerned and may be hoping that this story has a happy ending for Joanne. Please keep noticing your own thoughts, feelings and actions as you read on, as they will affect how you make sense of this story in your own life.

What was my reaction as I listened to Joanne? Some years ago I would probably have been on the 'Isn't she blessed to have two healthy boys?' side. Now, though, I see it as a huge privilege for me that she trusts me and confides the extent of her distress. My focus in on understanding as best I can what is going on for her. I no longer feel uncomfortable when someone like Joanne cries in my presence: I welcome those tears as a sign that the person is releasing some internal pressure, and I no longer see the need for me to help them to stop crying. I trust the tears and trust that they flow for a reason.

'Please make me feel better.' Those words resonate deeply, as few of us want to feel worse. Often when I meet people for the first time I explain that I see my work with them as being similar to working with people who have had a physical wound.

If I went for a walk and hurt my arm in a way that I didn't feel proud of I would automatically cover it up and pretend that the wound was not there. That approach might fool other people, and might even fool myself for a while, but sooner or later I would know that it's not getting better and I would go to someone to get my wound seen to. Help would involve taking the bandage off, which would probably hurt. The wound would need to be cleaned, which would also hurt; then antiseptic ointment might be applied, which could hurt even more. The final step would be to either leave the wound open so that it would heal naturally or for it to be gently wrapped up. Either way, it's vital that the wound is given a chance to heal, and not be picked at.

Now, listening to Joanne telling her story I would probably think of the courage it might have taken for her to come for help. I would feel humbled that she had chosen to tell her story to me, and I would acknowledge her tears and how difficult it might have been for her to tell me this. I might tell her my idea about the wound and explain that sometimes telling her story as she has done, with openness and honesty, is like pulling off a bandage.

At this point she might actually feel worse than she did before she came in. I would explore with her and find out if she was willing for me to show her a model based on CBT that I have developed to help people make sense of their feelings, to become aware of their thoughts and beliefs and to explore what they can do to improve things for themselves. Then, if she agreed, I would ask Joanne to choose something that was bothering her that she would like help with, and we would do the first step of the Coping Triangle together.

Fig. 3.1 shows the thoughts, feelings and actions that Joanne had in relation to her wanting to be the mother of a baby girl.

Fig. 3.1: Step 1 of Joanne's Coping Triangle

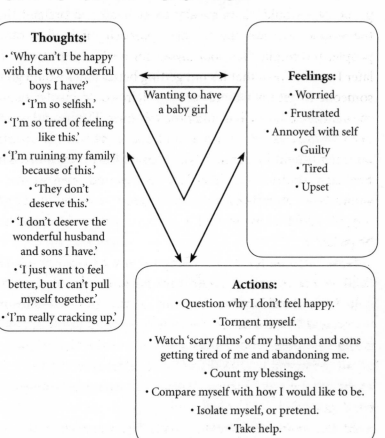

Thoughts:
- 'Why can't I be happy with the two wonderful boys I have?'
- 'I'm so selfish.'
- 'I'm so tired of feeling like this.'
- 'I'm ruining my family because of this.'
- 'They don't deserve this.'
- 'I don't deserve the wonderful husband and sons I have.'
- 'I just want to feel better, but I can't pull myself together.'
- 'I'm really cracking up.'

Wanting to have a baby girl

Feelings:
- Worried
- Frustrated
- Annoyed with self
- Guilty
- Tired
- Upset

Actions:
- Question why I don't feel happy.
- Torment myself.
- Watch 'scary films' of my husband and sons getting tired of me and abandoning me.
- Count my blessings.
- Compare myself with how I would like to be.
- Isolate myself, or pretend.
- Take help.

The process of doing step 1 was easy enough for Joanne, as she was very clear about what she was thinking and doing and how she was feeling. When I asked her what it was like to do this process she looked at me sadly and said, 'I already knew that I'm such a selfish woman, and this has made me even more aware of it.' I could practically hear her thinking, 'So this is not going to help me feel better.' I explained that while sometimes the process of doing the first of the three steps of the Coping Triangle can be a relief, often it could actually make a person feel worse as they begin to judge themselves even more harshly for feeling how they feel in the first place. Joanne nodded in agreement, as she was doing exactly that.

At this point I showed her the third finger of my left hand. I have two scars on that finger, and it is very slightly crooked. No-one would notice the scars or the crookedness if I didn't point them out. When I was ten years old, younger children were playing with razor blades. A friend and I took the blades from them and threw them away. I sliced three of my fingers with one of the blades as I threw it. A visit to the GP led me to meet a surgeon, who told my mother and me that the blade had cut the bone and the tendon of my third finger. He explained that I might never be able to bend that finger again or that it could remain bent and that I might never straighten it again.

He was an excellent surgeon and, thanks to his skill, my finger bends and straightens easily. For six months following the surgery however, my wound did not heal: it regularly flared into a mound of pus, which I would burst with a sterilised needle. One day I noticed that there was a black spot in the centre of my wound. The nurse who removed the stitches following the surgery had left one behind; as a result my wound had not healed. I required a second operation so that the surgeon could dig down and remove that stitch. Then my wound healed.

I often use the story of my crooked finger to illustrate how difficult, if not impossible, it can be for any of us to simply 'get on with life' if there is a wound or upset that is refusing to heal. I see the process of step 1 of the Coping Triangle as similar to the surgeon going beyond the skin to see what is causing the difficulties. It's lovely when someone finds step 1 a relief to do, but often it can actually make people feel worse as they become aware of what they feel, how they think and what they do. Given that many of us are so self-critical anyway, it's probably not surprising that discovering thoughts we don't like makes us judge ourselves harshly.

Also, it is important to mention here that some people tell me that they feel nothing when they do step 1, as they don't expect it to work anyway! This is fine too, as the point of step 1 is simply to find out what someone is thinking, feeling and doing, rather than to make them feel better!

Now back to Joanne and question 1 of step 2 of the Coping Triangle: Do Joanne's feelings make sense?

Immediately I asked her that question she looked at me in a troubled way and said, 'No, they don't make sense, but I just can't seem to stop feeling that way.' I then explained that if she had told me that she 'felt wonderful' because she thought that everyone she knew would consider her to be selfish to want a daughter and that she 'felt brilliant' because she worried that this might lead to the end of her marriage I would be concerned about her! I saw Joanne's feelings as making sense in that she didn't have what she wanted and in how she was thinking and how she was feeling. An important thing, though, was that Joanne judged herself according to her feelings, and because she didn't feel good she considered that there was something inherently flawed about her.

I see Joanne's feelings as responding to her thoughts and actions in exactly the same way that a three-year-old child might respond to an adult. Three-year-old children are absolutely wonderful. We know exactly where we stand with them; we'll know if they feel tired, hungry, upset, left out, or jealous. Picture yourself going to the zoo with a three-year-old. For whatever reason, you're not in the humour to see the child run off excitedly to look at the many things that capture their attention. You snap, 'Don't run off like that! I told you that you had to be good,' and the child begins to cry. Or you go into the zoo holding on to the child's hand so tightly that there is no possibility that they are going to escape. 'Don't let go of my hand: it's too busy today. We should have come on a different day. If you get lost I'll never find you!' How could we be surprised if the three-year-old begins to feel anxious!

How does this fit in with Joanne? She labelled her feelings 'bad'. Certainly they were distressing and painful, but why were they 'bad'? When I asked her this question she shrugged helplessly and said, 'I shouldn't feel like this when I have so much going for me, particularly as I have two gorgeous sons.' So we wrote that in the 'thoughts' section, recognising the guilt that this thought generated.

How would life be for Joanne, I wondered with her, if she didn't know that having a daughter was so important for her? Could there possibly be anything good in the fact that she was feeling so awful? Joanne turned to look at me and said, with a hint of wonder, 'If I didn't feel this bad I wouldn't be here. I wouldn't be looking at this, and I would probably go on pretending that I'm fine.'

Joanne's response answers the question 'What's good about feeling bad?' If we see our feelings—all of them—as messengers inviting us to respond, then we can step back from blaming, judging, hiding, apologising and worrying because we have them. If we can begin to see our feelings just as we would those of a three-year-old child, like Anna in chapter 1, we can begin to show ourselves the same compassion that we would instinctively feel for a little child who is feeling frightened, upset, left out, alone or hurt.

So what was good about Joanne feeling bad? Her feelings were letting her know, very clearly and persistently, that she needed to examine her thoughts, her actions and the meaning for her of not having a daughter. Far from being the terrible things she had seen them as being, they were in fact wonderful and were very much to be welcomed! As Rumi wrote many years ago,

> The dark thought, the shame, the malice,
> meet them at the door laughing,
> and invite them in.

At this point you may be thinking, 'It's not that easy,' so let's look at that!

Chapter 4
Do you think it's not that easy?

Be grateful for whoever comes,
because each has been sent
as a guide from beyond.

—MEWLANA JALALUDDIN RUMI

D o you remember the Numskulls? They were wonderful characters in the *Beano* comics (and if you've no idea who they were you can still enjoy their wisdom and simplicity on the internet). I felt sorry for them as they worked so hard in their owner's head, enacting scenes that the person was 'watching'. If the person turned the switch to tennis, the Numskulls would quickly don white T-shirts and shorts and play tennis. If moments later the person decided that tennis was too slow to watch and that a football match would be more entertaining, the remote control would be switched again.

Picture the Numskulls quickly changing the scene, recruiting more characters, making sure they're in appropriate football gear, and going out to play. Of course the remote control kept being switched and the scene kept changing, over and over and over. The initial fun of the tennis match very quickly turned into pressure.

Does this seem familiar? My head often reminds me of the Numskulls. Sometimes I feel sorry for my thoughts as they jump around my head, frightened and lost. At other times they annoy and frustrate me—particularly if I'm supposed to be asleep! Thoughts can shock, surprise, upset, taunt, worry and torture us. Yes, some thoughts are wonderful: we may be feeling tired, hungry or frustrated and then open a door, smell freshly baked bread and think, 'Mmmm.' Immediately we can feel some sense of peace as our thoughts create a film in our head of a time in our past when someone we loved baked bread. This wonderful thought may be followed almost immediately by 'I miss her so much,' and suddenly we feel sad; the thought may instead be followed by 'I love the smell of freshly baked bread,' which may then be followed by a sense of hope and anticipation and the thought 'I hope there'll be some for me!'

So much of what we do, how we feel and who we are depends on what we think. Some thoughts can be interesting, exciting, challenging, and some can be frightening and upsetting. Even with all the advances in technology and the increased know-ledge we have, few if any of us have full control over our thoughts. They can suddenly appear and take us by surprise.

Recently a constant pain in one of my teeth convinced me to make an appointment to see my dentist. The relief I felt when I phoned and spoke to the receptionist was swiftly and unexpect-edly ruined by a thought that barged into my head unannounced and unwelcome and causing me upset. 'What will you do,' this thought tortured me, 'when your dentist retires?' Hopefully my dentist has many more years to go before he decides to take a well-earned rest from working in his surgery. Logically I know that there are many skilled, talented and caring professionals whom I could trust to care for my teeth, but I wasn't thinking about them: instead I was experiencing a moment of loss, confusion and distress.

It really is a bit mad, and we can see why mindfulness is so popular. It encourages us to stay in the present and not react to distressing thoughts. At that moment I had no defence, though. It was bad enough to have a very sore tooth; as a result of that

thought I was suddenly spiralled into a future of sore teeth and
no dentist!

● Dr Aaron Beck is an American psychiatrist who is world-
renowned for developing cognitive behavioural therapy. He was
a trained psychoanalyst, so he had the benefit of listening to his
patients speaking their thoughts out loud for hours and hours.
At some point, or so the story goes, he noticed an expression on
a woman's face that didn't seem to match what she was saying.
He asked her what she was thinking. She answered: 'I was
thinking you must be tired of listening to me saying all this.'

● Dr Beck realised that she was telling him one thing and yet
thinking something very different, and he began to focus on
what she was actually thinking: her thoughts or, to give them
another word, her cognitions. He discovered quite quickly that
if he gave his attention to what his patients thought and did, as
opposed to how they felt, they made huge improvements in
their general well-being in a very short time. He began to
evaluate the effectiveness of his practice, and to teach others,
and very quickly CBT was born.

Dr Beck's timing was perfect, as his work built on the
excellent research of other people, such as Dr Albert Bandura,
Dr Albert Ellis and Dr Carl Rogers. Bandura's work demonstrated that we are influenced more by what people do than by
what they say. His experiment on how children responded to
adults aggressively hitting Bobo the doll is well worth watching
on Youtube.

Albert Ellis dealt with whether thoughts are rational or
irrational. His therapy, 'rational emotive behavioural therapy'
(REBT), dealt particularly with challenging core beliefs.

Some people who may be critical of CBT, describing it as a
'quick fix', may be surprised that I have included Carl Rogers as
having been influential in the development of CBT. Rogers is
known best for the emphasis he placed on developing a strong

therapeutic relationship through treating people with respect and what he described as unconditional positive regard. Thanks to the treasure trove that is the internet we can watch Carl Rogers and Albert Ellis demonstrating their respective approaches in responding to the needs of a woman in distress, recorded in 1965. While it's easy to see which of the therapists Gloria preferred, I am still fascinated to watch how Ellis is able to get her to stop and question her own thinking.

I would strongly encourage you to watch a third video, which is only eight minutes long, in which Aaron Beck talks about the influences of Ellis and Rogers as well as another psychologist, Dr George Kelly, on his own work.

Professor Philip Kendall was one of the first people to adopt CBT in his work with children and adolescents, and I was fortunate to be trained by him in 1998.

Over the past thirty-five years other people have built on Beck's ideas, and we are now in what has become known as the 'Third Age of CBT'. This includes developments in acceptance commitment therapy (ACT) and mindfulness. ACT was developed by Dr Stephen Hayes and his colleagues.

Jon Kabat-Zinn is recognised as one of the most important people to bring mindfulness to the Western world and to research its effectiveness. Many lectures and presentations that he has given are available on the internet; one that you might like to watch first is his lecture in Google in 2011.

The emphasis has now changed from encouraging people to challenge their thoughts to gently and compassionately acknowledging that they are there. Mindfulness has now also been proved to be an effective treatment for a range of difficulties and is recommended to help prevent a recurrence of severe depression. Many excellent books have been written using the principles of CBT to help people cope with a range of difficulties, such as depression, anxiety, low self-esteem and OCD.

The Welcoming Approach invites us to welcome thoughts into our awareness so that we can do something about them. Have you ever left home to go on a journey thinking that you have forgotten something? If you have you may well have experienced the physical feelings of some anxiety (sick feeling, tightness in your chest and sense of dread), and it's likely that you spent a few moments working your way through a mental check-list to see if you can remember what it is. Did you turn off the lights? lock the door? tell the neighbours you were leaving? I love the feeling of relief when I realise I've forgotten to pack a towel and immediately think, 'It's all right: I can get one when I get there.' So welcoming that thought—'I forgot to pack a towel'—frees me to concentrate on what I can do about it.

When I talk to people about thoughts I often ask them not to think of something such as a beautiful sunset, or someone burning toast, or a bus pulling out of the bus stop just as they arrive. As you may already have noticed, it's actually impossible for us not to think. As soon as we put energy into *not* thinking about something, we think about it. This can be frustrating, exhausting and difficult for people who have a lot of recurrent thoughts that cause them distress.

I invite you to view thoughts differently. See yourself walking into your kitchen. You notice four strangers sitting there. They're wearing dirty clothes and are clearly unwashed, and two look as if they're injecting themselves with something. As you walk in, one of the four turns towards you and says, 'It's about time someone arrived. We'll have a cup of tea.' What would you do?

While some people have told me that they would question the men about who they are, almost everyone sooner or later gets to the point where they would ask them to leave. They would recognise that they don't want them there, and they would take steps to get rid of them.

On rare occasions I have met people who tell me that their first instinct would be to make them tea, give them dinner and even offer them a bed for the night. When I ask what they think they would do three weeks later if the people are still there, they are clear that they would then ask them to leave. I have met one person though who told me that he actually did walk into his kitchen and saw strangers sitting there. He was curious about who they were and welcomed them to stay as long as they wanted. When I talk about the Welcoming Approach I am not suggesting that any of us go that far!

I see our thoughts being like strangers in our kitchen. Some strangers we recognise immediately as being potentially dangerous and we know that we don't want them to be there; other strangers may present themselves in a more subtle way but may also be harmful. An example of this may be someone who is well dressed and charming who has been invited into your home by a member of your family but your instincts scream at you that there is something not right. We have all heard stories about people who have been cruelly taken advantage of by people they first trusted and invited into their home.

It's easy enough to recognise some thoughts we may have as dangerous, but other thoughts may be true and may seem helpful but may actually be extremely destructive. Dr Aaron Beck described thoughts as 'positive' or 'negative'; Dr David Burns, in his book *Feeling Good: The New Mood Therapy* (1980), expanded on this to describe thoughts as 'cognitive distortions', classifying them as different types, including filtering, polarised or 'black-and-white' thinking, overgeneralisation and 'catastrophising'. Dr Tony Bates worked with both Beck and Burns, and his book *Coming Through Depression: A Mindful Approach* (2011) illustrates how clinicians have moved from helping people to classify their thoughts to becoming aware of them and responding to them mindfully.

My work with people who have OCD has shown me that, while labelling thoughts with one of the categories of cognitive distortions may be beneficial for some people, it could actually exacerbate difficulties for others, if they become obsessive in labelling their thoughts correctly. Some years ago I began to help people recognise their thoughts and then simply see if they were 'helpful' or 'unhelpful'. I see an important distinction between these two words and the words 'positive' and 'negative'. The example I've used many times is to ask, 'If you were on an aeroplane, up in the air, and the door falls off, a positive thought might be "Oh, we're getting some fresh air in"; but is it helpful?' Many of us have felt pressured to 'think positively' even when faced with huge difficulties and challenges. This doesn't seem fair, can create extra pressure and, as Dr Martin Seligman has demonstrated in his work on optimism, can actually increase difficulties.

Let's look again at Stephen. He's the man who had the heart transplant whom we met in chapter 2. You may remember that he became extremely distressed because he didn't feel happy afterwards. Fig. 4.1 shows his first step in the Coping Triangle, which was to capture his thoughts, his feelings and his actions in relation to something that's concerning him. In Stephen's case he was mostly concerned with himself and his reaction to having had his transplant. The second step is to ask the four questions. We know from chapter 2 that the answer to the first one—'Do Stephen's feelings make sense?'—is Yes. They make sense because of the reality of his heart transplant and because of what he's thinking and what he's doing.

Let's turn now to look at the second question: 'Are his thoughts helpful or unhelpful?' See what you think. If you consider a thought helpful place the letter H beside it and if unhelpful the letter U.

Fig. 4.1: Are Stephen's thoughts 'helpful' or 'unhelpful'?

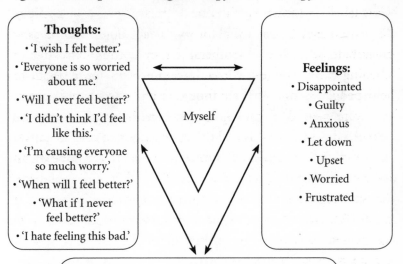

Thoughts:
- 'I wish I felt better.'
- 'Everyone is so worried about me.'
- 'Will I ever feel better?'
- 'I didn't think I'd feel like this.'
- 'I'm causing everyone so much worry.'
- 'When will I feel better?'
- 'What if I never feel better?'
- 'I hate feeling this bad.'

Myself

Feelings:
- Disappointed
- Guilty
- Anxious
- Let down
- Upset
- Worried
- Frustrated

Actions:
- Concentrate on my feelings of distress.
- Compare how I feel with how I used to feel and how I expected to feel.
- Tell others how I feel.
- Blame myself and others for not feeling better.
- Replay times when I felt better.
- Anticipate feeling even worse.

Let's look at Stephen's thoughts one at time. His thought *'I wish I felt better'* is absolutely true: he really does wish that he felt better. Is it a 'helpful thought', though? I consider it unhelpful, for several reasons. The first is that when he thinks *'I wish I felt better'* he immediately feels the distress of *not* feeling better. I see it as unhelpful also, because there's an assumption that there's something wrong with not feeling better, and this can put more pressure on him. Often thoughts are like carriages on a train, one pulling another. The thought *'I wish I felt better'* may immediately lead to another thought, *'Because I don't like feeling how I'm feeling,'* which in turn can contribute to Stephen feeling even worse!

'Everyone is so worried about me' is a thought that Stephen automatically thinks is true; and when he thinks this he feels guilty. This on its own is sufficient reason for it to be an unhelpful thought; but is it in fact true? Is it true that everyone, absolutely everyone on the planet, is worried about him? Put like that, of course it's not. However, Stephen would be unlikely to question that thought: if he did he would know immediately that not everyone worries about him, as most people don't know him! It may well be, though, that some people who do know him may not in fact be worried about him, such as the medical team that carried out his surgery.

'Will I ever feel better?' is what I call a 'question-thought'. Some question-thoughts can be very helpful. For instance, if I sleep it out some morning and then ask myself, 'Why did I sleep it out?' and take action to discover that the batteries in my alarm clock need to be replaced, and then replace them, that question-thought is helpful. If, however, I ask myself, 'Why do people drop litter on the ground?' I could easily get into a downward spiral of feeling annoyed, aggrieved and even hopeless. That thought is not helpful, unless it encourages me to take steps to see, for example, if some litter bins could be installed.

What about Stephen's question-thought *'Will I ever feel better?'* I see this as unhelpful, as when Stephen thinks it he immediately feels anxious, as he projects himself into a time in the future when he will not feel good. I also see it as unhelpful because that thought invites in other unhelpful thoughts, such as *'What if I don't feel better?' 'I hate feeling this bad,'* and *'I'm frightened that I'll never feel better.'* Each of those thoughts in turn then prompts Stephen to feel even worse.

Fig. 4.2: Are Stephen's thoughts 'helpful' or 'unhelpful'?

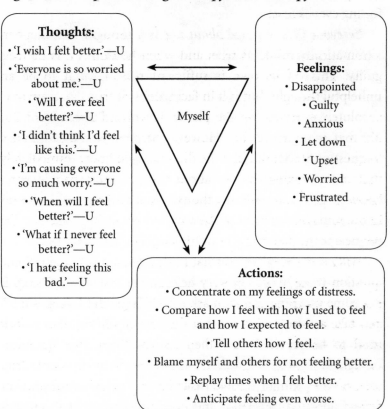

Thoughts:
- 'I wish I felt better.'—U
- 'Everyone is so worried about me.'—U
- 'Will I ever feel better?'—U
- 'I didn't think I'd feel like this.'—U
- 'I'm causing everyone so much worry.'—U
- 'When will I feel better?'—U
- 'What if I never feel better?'—U
- 'I hate feeling this bad.'—U

Myself

Feelings:
- Disappointed
- Guilty
- Anxious
- Let down
- Upset
- Worried
- Frustrated

Actions:
- Concentrate on my feelings of distress.
- Compare how I feel with how I used to feel and how I expected to feel.
- Tell others how I feel.
- Blame myself and others for not feeling better.
- Replay times when I felt better.
- Anticipate feeling even worse.

The thought *'I didn't think I'd feel like this'* is true. It's unhelpful for Stephen, as it causes him to concentrate on how distressed he's feeling. Telling himself that he's 'causing everyone so much worry' is not helpful either, as it doesn't make him feel good and instead can make him feel guilty, upset and a burden.

His next thought, 'When will I feel better?' is another question-thought and is also unhelpful. He doesn't know when he will feel better, thus causing him to feel anxious and worried. This quickly leads to his next thought, *'What if I never feel better?'* This causes him to feel even more anxious and more worried and is also unhelpful. Asking himself if he will ever feel better can trigger a sense of hopelessness and fear as he pictures himself never feeling better.

Stephen's final thought, *'I hate feeling this bad,'* is absolutely true. He does hate feeling bad. But he knows this already, and so he doesn't need a thought marching around his head reminding him and making him feel even worse.

Fig. 4.2 shows how the thought section in Stephen's Coping Triangle looks after he asks himself whether his thoughts are 'helpful' or 'unhelpful'.

At this point I often ask people, 'What is it like to have gone through each of your thoughts to see if they are helpful or unhelpful?' While some people find this a relief, many find it very difficult to do. They immediately blame themselves for having so many unhelpful thoughts and may feel overwhelmed and embarrassed by them. I tend to write down those thoughts and then ask them if they are 'helpful' or 'unhelpful' too! You can see how we could keep going round and round; and if that's all we did we could end up in a worse position than when we began!

The Welcoming Approach doesn't end here, though. Rather than fighting with or judging thoughts we don't like we learn to gently see them for what they are: unhelpful. That frees us to explore what is driving the thoughts in the first place: our beliefs, which we will look at in the next chapter. For now, I invite you to look at your own thoughts in fig. 4.3 and ask yourself whether each one is helpful or unhelpful.

It's important that you know why. Sometimes thoughts may be unhelpful because of how they cause us to feel. I often think of thoughts as if they are adults and feelings as if they are three-year-old children. Picture a little boy or girl running excitedly to an adult to show them a picture they have just drawn. Now imagine the child's reaction if the adult says in a sarcastic tone of voice, 'Is that the best you can do?'

We wouldn't be surprised at all to know that the child responds directly to the adult without questioning whether the adult is actually unkind, having a bad day, or simply not a good judge of drawing. Children tend to accept what adults say. Our feelings can respond to our thoughts in a similar way. If we think, 'Here's another fine mess I've made of things,' how could we expect to feel good about ourselves?

Fig. 4.3: Are My thoughts helpful or unhelpful?

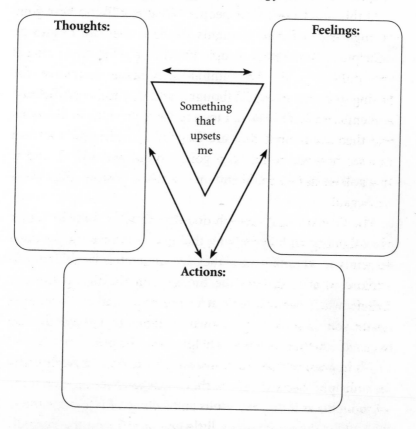

As you look at your own thoughts and consider how helpful or unhelpful they are, how will you respond to Rumi's invitation?

Welcome and entertain them all!
Even if they're a crowd of sorrows,
who violently sweep your house
empty of its furniture,
still treat each guest honourably.
He may be clearing you out
for some new delight.
Every morning a new arrival.

The chances are that you will be even more distressed by the
idea that you welcome your thoughts and treat them honourably. Yet Rumi goes even further: he encourages us to

Be grateful for whoever comes,
because each has been sent
as a guide from beyond.

Speaking from experience, I know it can be very difficult to
welcome some thoughts as anything, let alone as a guide from
beyond. How many times have I been on the point of sleep
when I'm cruelly interrupted by a thought taunting me that,
despite my best intentions, I still haven't done what I intended
to do that day. I've noticed that such thoughts tend to have
more power to distress me when I'm feeling tired or vulnerable.
People who have OCD can find such thoughts particularly distressing. They can range from 'You didn't lock the front door'
to 'You coughed in someone's face and may have given them
an infection.'
     Such thoughts are cruel and can be deeply distressing. I have
found that arguing back at them tends not to work; instead,
simply recognising them as 'unhelpful' can free us to concentrate on how we are going to respond to them, which is the
subject of chapter 6.

Perhaps the most upsetting thoughts for some people, though, are the thoughts that they 'are better off dead,' that 'other people would be better off if they are dead,' that 'they don't deserve to live' and that 'there's no point.' These thoughts can be extremely distressing and frightening. Often they are followed by a thought that 'I'm suicidal.'

Over the past few years I have deliberately drawn a clear distinction between thoughts such as these, which I consider unhelpful, and the action of someone choosing to take their own life. It's vitally important for all of us to step back from the emotive language of suicide and realise that just because people think they are better off dead doesn't mean they are suicidal. Such thoughts are probably a lot more common than we know. Also, the fact that someone thinks thoughts such as these doesn't mean they have to act on them in a way that harms themselves or others.

Has anyone ever told you to 'just stop thinking about it'? It's now well known and accepted that this is actually impossible. We can't 'not think'. Ask people not to think of a daffodil and, despite their best efforts, they'll do just that; ask them then not to think of twenty daffodils in a field by a lake, with two swans swimming, and they may smile as they picture this lovely scene. Then, to make really sure they've got the point, ask them not to think of a herd of cows running down the field, flattening the daffodils, and the swans flying away in surprise. At this point I would hope they might laugh.

It's impossible not to think. The more we try not to think certain thoughts the more power they have to charge around our heads uninvited. I don't know precisely what thoughts are; I see them like the Numskulls, though: little characters, with their own unique personalities. Some are very young and may speak, cry or whine in a babyish voice. Such thoughts as 'Why me?' 'It's not fair' and 'I want more' may be very young. Depending on the tone, these thoughts may scream at us like sulky teenagers. We may even have more angry 'teenager thoughts', such as 'Leave me alone,' 'I hate this' and 'It's all your fault.' We tend to respond to real children and teenagers much more appropriately than we often do to our thoughts. Good parenting encourages us to be realistic about how angelic and perfect we need to be as adults striving to cope with the constant demands of young people. We generally adopt one of a few possible approaches, depending on what seems to fit best at that time.

Thoughts are thoughts. They can be helpful or they can be unhelpful. Unhelpful thoughts can cause us to feel anxious, frightened, upset, worried, embarrassed and a whole range of other emotions. They are still only thoughts, though. Welcoming them into our awareness is important, so that we can realise exactly what they are telling us, rather than letting them whisper away in a quiet, vindictive way. We then have an opportunity to recognise our thoughts for what they are: thoughts.

Thoughts, no matter how awful they seem, cannot do us any harm unless we actually believe them! Think it's not that easy? Well, maybe it is!

Chapter 5
Maybe it is that easy: 'What we believe is true'

No matter what they tell us
No matter what they do
No matter what they teach us
What we believe is true.

—JIM STEINMAN

Maybe it is that easy. Maybe we can feel at peace with ourselves and others by welcoming our feelings of distress as messengers.

Take a few moments to read those lines from the song 'No Matter What', written by Jim Steinman with music by Andrew Lloyd Webber for the musical *Whistle Down the Wind*, which also became a huge hit for the boy band Boyzone.

As the words of the song gently swirl around my head I'm reminded of the many people I have had the privilege to work with who believed terrible things about themselves. Many believed that they were stupid; practically all believed at some level that they were not good enough; some even believed they were unlovable. I realised quickly that I couldn't convince them that they were bright, good enough or lovable—in fact the more I tried the more entrenched they became in their belief. I was in danger of falling into the trap of becoming yet another person who had 'failed' to make them feel better.

Dr Albert Ellis's work has been very influential in helping people to dispute what he referred to as irrational beliefs. These include such beliefs as 'I must do well and win the approval of others or else I'm no good'; 'other people must do the "right thing" or else they're no good and deserve to be punished'; and 'life must be easy, without discomfort or inconvenience.' Many books have been published by Ellis and others on 'rational emotive behaviour therapy' (REBT). Among the many web sites I found, the REBT Network (www.rebtnetwork.org) is particularly comprehensive. Many years after Ellis became well known and respected for his work another American, Byron Katie, discovered that her experience of severe depression was a result of her beliefs about how her life should be. She found that a technique of inquiry that she called 'the Work' was effective in challenging her beliefs and in changing her thinking. I have read many of her books and have also attended a seminar at which she demonstrated how asking four crucial questions can affect what people believe about their circumstances. There are numerous sites on the internet that refer to Byron Katie's work, but the essential one is www.thework.com.

The Welcoming Approach differs from both Albert Ellis's and Byron Katie's work in that it doesn't ask you to challenge what you believe: instead, question 3 of step 2 simply asks you to become aware of what you believe and realise that the fact that you believe it doesn't make it true. Epictetus was a Greek philosopher who wrote in approximately AD 100 that it is not our thoughts but the meaning of our thoughts that causes us distress; the meaning tends to come from what we believe.

Let's look at a fictitious example that almost all of us can relate to in one way or another. Think of yourself at the age of fifteen walking down a corridor in your school. You notice a group of your classmates at the end of the corridor laughing, and as you approach, one of them turns and sees you, and suddenly they all stop laughing. What might you immediately and automatically think? The most common answer I have received is 'They were talking about me.'

Well, let's suppose that's true and that they were talking about you. What difference would that make to you? What effect would it have on your life? The answer to that question depends not on what you think but on the meaning of that thought, which originates from beliefs you developed when you were very young that are called our 'core beliefs'.

This is easy enough to see if you think of six different people who have been in the same situation and who have thought, 'They're talking about me.' One of the people immediately feels sad and wishes that they weren't there.

The second person thinks, 'They're talking about me,' which thought is quickly followed by 'Why? Is it something I did? What will I do now? Will I pretend I didn't see them? But if they know that I saw them and then I pretend that I didn't I'll seem even more stupid.' Not surprisingly, that person will feel anxious and will probably avoid meeting the others by either turning around or taking a detour.

Person 3 will think, 'They're talking about me,' then will think, 'How dare they!' and feel angry and will march up to them and confront them.

'They're talking about me? Brilliant!' the fourth person will think, making an assumption that the others are discussing how fantastic he or she played in a school game the previous evening! I sometimes joke that person 4 is destined to become a politician, who thinks everyone is talking about them and that that's great!

Person 5 will think, 'They're talking about me,' in a curious way that doesn't cause them to feel any distress.

If you're thinking that not everyone would jump to the conclusion that people are talking about them, you're right. The last person would immediately follow the thought 'They're talking about me' with another thought such as 'Maybe they're not.'

So what's going on in these situations to drive the different responses these six people have to the exact same thought? It wasn't the thought 'They're talking about me': instead it was the meaning of the thought, which differed for each of them according to what they believed. And to think that Epictetus knew this more than two thousand years ago!

Let's look again at Joanne's story and see if we can understand what belief or beliefs may have been driving her to have such a distressed reaction to thinking that she wanted to have a baby daughter. Fig. 5.1 shows the first step of her Coping Triangle, which was to catch what she was thinking, how she was feeling and what she was doing in relation to her concern about wanting to have a daughter. Step 2 is for her to ask herself four questions. (We looked at the first of these in chapter 3 and saw that her feelings do make sense because of how she blames herself for wanting to have a baby girl and because of her very harsh thoughts.)

If you look at each of her thoughts and ask the second question, 'Are her thoughts helpful or unhelpful?' you might agree with me that they are all unhelpful. Anyone who is as self-critical as Joanne might disagree and say that the thought 'Why can't I be happy with the two wonderful boys that I have?' is very helpful. It may be if it triggered a sense of peace and gratitude for being the mother of two boys; for Joanne, though, that question-thought has no answer. She doesn't know why she can't be happy, even though she has two boys. This prompts her to worry about this, to become frustrated, and then the harsh and judgemental thought 'I'm so selfish' appears and causes her to feel even worse.

Fig. 5.1: Joanne's Coping Triangle

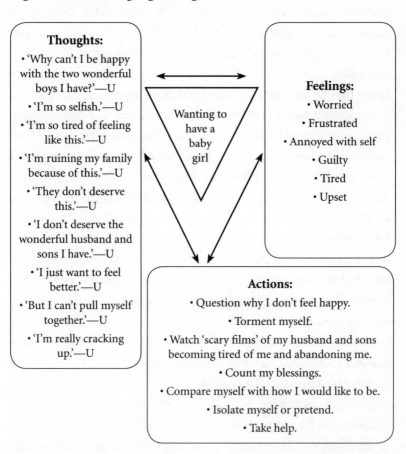

Thoughts:
- 'Why can't I be happy with the two wonderful boys I have?'—U
- 'I'm so selfish.'—U
- 'I'm so tired of feeling like this.'—U
- 'I'm ruining my family because of this.'—U
- 'They don't deserve this.'—U
- 'I don't deserve the wonderful husband and sons I have.'—U
- 'I just want to feel better.'—U
- 'But I can't pull myself together.'—U
- 'I'm really cracking up.'—U

Wanting to have a baby girl

Feelings:
- Worried
- Frustrated
- Annoyed with self
- Guilty
- Tired
- Upset

Actions:
- Question why I don't feel happy.
- Torment myself.
- Watch 'scary films' of my husband and sons becoming tired of me and abandoning me.
- Count my blessings.
- Compare myself with how I would like to be.
- Isolate myself or pretend.
- Take help.

What do you think Joanne actually believes? If you were her best friend and are a woman you may listen sympathetically over and over. You may do your best to convince her that she's fine as she is. However, I predict that you'll end up feeling frustrated as, despite your best efforts, Joanne will still feel distressed. If you're a man whom Joanne has confided in you would probably listen compassionately the first, second and perhaps third time. After listening you might go into 'fix it' mode and suggest a solution for Joanne's dilemma. You might suggest that her options are as follows:

1. Tell her husband that she wants a baby girl and that she's going to keep getting pregnant until she has one.
2. Adopt a baby girl.
3. Decide that she's not going to get pregnant again.

If you are a 'typical man' (if such a thing exists!) you may feel good while having this conversation. You are present, you are listening, and you may well think that you are helping. The snag is that reassurance doesn't work. When, despite your best efforts, Joanne still feels upset you may feel frustrated as you think, 'Why will she not just accept what she has and get on with her life?' Depending on your own level of self-confidence, regardless of whether you are a man or a woman, you may think you haven't done enough to help her and may feel something of a failure.

So how might the Welcoming Approach help Joanne? There is obviously something driving her to feel so terrible. Rather than problem-solving or listening to her telling us how guilty she feels, let's see if we can understand what is actually so bad for Joanne about not having a baby girl. It's a bit like seeing the elephant in the room. There is a technique that I was trained in, developed by Dr David Burns, called 'Socratic Questioning' or the 'Downward Arrow'. This can be very useful in uncovering core beliefs. Let's ask Joanne simply, 'What's so bad about wanting to have a daughter?' She may say, 'Because I have two healthy sons.' Then we ask, 'What's so bad about having two healthy sons and still wanting a daughter?' Fig. 5.2 shows us where this might take us.

Fig. 5.2: *Uncovering Joanne's core belief about wanting a daughter*

	I have no daughter.
What's so bad about not having a daughter?	↓
	I have two healthy sons.
What's so bad about having two healthy sons and not having a daughter?	↓
	I want a daughter too.
What's so bad about wanting a daughter too?	↓
	I'm not supposed to want things.

At this point I wouldn't be surprised if Joanne had an 'Oh, my gosh!' reaction as she realises how her belief that she is not supposed to want things suddenly makes sense to her. She might relate this to her experience of having wanted a younger sister when she was growing up and learning that her wishes were unacceptable and caused other people problems. We can all grow up with mixed messages and somehow learn that to be acceptable, valuable and worthy we must not want anything for ourselves.

I am blessed to have very special children in my life. One of my most powerful teachers has been my niece Róisín, from the moment I first saw her when she was two hours old. One of my lessons was when she was four years old and she was skipping beside me as we walked through a shopping centre. She suddenly saw something that she liked and said she wanted it. Automatically I said, 'I know you do, but you can't have it.'

This response usually worked for me with anything that I wanted and knew I wasn't getting. It didn't work, though, for this gorgeous, determined little person, who deep down knew that it actually was all right, not wrong, to want something. After hearing me automatically respond to her by saying the same thing at least three times, she stopped walking, turned to face me and in a clear, no-nonsense voice told me: 'Claire, I want it.'

I can still remember my reaction of amazement that it was actually all right for her, and for me, to want something and to say that we want it. This doesn't necessarily mean that we will get it, but if we ignore the sense of wanting something it can actually turn into resentment.

From that point on I began to be a little kinder to myself about my own wants, rather than cruelly giving out to myself for 'wanting more' and reminding myself to 'count my blessings.'

So I can relate to how Joanne might respond, though her response would be different from mine, yours, and everyone else's. Joanne's response would be related to the specific meaning for her of not being supposed to want something. Her reaction to realising that she did believe, 100 per cent, that she was not allowed to want something confirmed that this was definitely a powerful and destructive core belief for her. When we explored at what point in her life she may have begun to believe that she was not allowed to want anything Joanne immediately described her mother's reaction to her request for a baby sister. She was a child and had no way of knowing that her innocent and understandable request might have caused her mother to feel a deep sense of pain. Now, as an adult, Joanne could compassionately see how difficult that request must have been for her mother.

It took a little longer for Joanne to see how she equated asking for something with causing pain for someone else. It was no wonder, then, that she struggled with asking for anything from then on. She smiled as she began to see all sorts of connections and patterns throughout her life that illustrated how powerful her core belief was. She explained that she had attended a training workshop some years previously and at the end the participants were divided into groups of four. They were directed to take turns in asking the others to do something nice for them. She said that she couldn't ask for anything and watched in dismay as the others asked for a hug, or a back rub, or a cup of coffee. She recalled thinking that they were all selfish for imposing their wants on others and was puzzled about why anyone would be encouraged to ask someone else for something that they wanted.

Core beliefs are indeed very powerful. If we don't know they are there they can cause a great deal of distress. Becoming aware of them is an important step in tackling them; but awareness on its own is sometimes not enough. I remember buying a book at an airport and reading the first two chapters a few hours later, thousands of feet up in the air. Perhaps it was being up so high that allowed me to see things from a new viewpoint, but I suddenly made a connection with the words I was reading and a deep core belief that I had not known was there but that had caused me so much trouble for years! The author of the book suggested that I reflect on my early experiences with my siblings and asked what messages I had picked up from them. I suddenly had a very clear memory of my two older brothers rushing me to eat my dinner quickly so that they could bring me back to school and then play football with their friends. They were seven and eight and I was four years old. The message I picked up was that I was a nuisance, and from my seat in the plane, miles up in the sky, I could see how that belief had influenced me so many times in my own life.

The timing of my uncovering that belief was also wonderful. Two days after I reached my destination I was in a situation where someone spent hours sharing his knowledge of a particular subject with me. I still remember how acutely uncomfortable I felt and how loudly thoughts in my head screamed at me to say goodbye and leave. *Did I not know how many other things he had to do instead of standing there talking to me?*

When I valiantly ignored that thought, other thoughts rushed in. *Who did I think I was to take up so much of that man's time?* and *He's only being kind and is too polite to ask me to leave.* Perhaps the most persistent thought was *Other people are noticing that you're still here and that you're taking up so much of his time.*

I felt more and more uncomfortable; but somehow, knowing that I had believed from when I was four years old that I was a nuisance helped me to question that belief. With almost every cell in my body screaming at me to say goodbye, thank him for his help and apologise for taking up so much of his time, I resisted by saying to myself over and over, *He is choosing to share this information with me, and maybe I'm not a nuisance.*

I discovered something then that I have used many times since. It doesn't work to battle against a core belief, because it can become even more ingrained. Instead the fabulous, gentle and ever so powerful word 'maybe' works. Managing to stay and resisting my urge to flee was a crucial moment in my life.

Often uncovering one core belief leads us to another, even deeper one. Let's use the Downward Arrow Technique to explore Joanne's core belief that she is not supposed to want things.

Fig. 5.3: Exploring Joanne's core belief about not being supposed to want things

	I'm not supposed to want things.
What's so bad about wanting things?	↓
	I should be happy with what I have.
What's so bad about not being happy with what you have?	↓
	I'm greedy and selfish.
What's so bad about being greedy and selfish?	↓
	Other people won't like me.
What's so bad about other people not liking you?	↓
	I'm not supposed to be selfish.
What's so bad about being selfish?	↓
	Other people will become annoyed.
What's so bad about other people becoming annoyed?	↓
	They'll become tired of me.
What's so bad about other people becoming tired of you?	↓
	I'll be on my own.
What's so bad about being on your own?	↓
	I'm not enough on my own.

What have you been thinking, and how have you been feeling, as you read Joanne's Downward Arrow Spiral? You may have thought, 'Oh, for goodness' sake, she's totally absorbed in herself and needs to grow up!' If so, you would probably have felt frustrated and irritated. You may, however, have had a thought such as 'I can relate to Joanne, as I sometimes think that I should be happy with what I have,' and perhaps feel some sympathy with her. Your feelings, whatever they are, would most probably make sense; though if you feel irritated as you read her story you may prefer not to feel that way!

Sometimes it can take time to discover why it is that we react to things in certain ways. Uncovering core beliefs can take time but can be very worth while. Joanne, for instance, had no idea that she believed she was 'not enough on her own.' When she began to reflect on her life she realised that she constantly strived and failed to 'be enough.' Logically she knew that her deep desire to have a sister had somehow influenced her to want to have a daughter. She was stunned, however, to realise that her desire was rooted in her own sense of unworthiness and of not being enough. As she began to reflect on the effect this core belief had on her whole life, the words someone had said to her when she was pregnant with her first child began to torture her. 'I hope you have a baby girl,' a colleague had said to her and quoted the old saying, 'A son is a son till he gets him a wife; a daughter's a daughter for the rest of her life.' Joanne hadn't realised how deeply those words had affected her and remembered now her brief moment of disappointment when she was told that she had a son.

Horrified, Joanne now began to challenge her core belief. Did she really think she was not enough on her own? How fair was it to expect a little girl to be born solely to make sure that her mother didn't feel inadequate? She wondered then how it would be if she went on to have six more boys. Would she begin to resent them for not being girls? With sudden clarity, Joanne realised that she didn't need someone else to be born and to live solely to make her feel that she was enough. With that realisation she gained instant peace as she decided that she was going to consider herself as 'more than enough' with or without a daughter.

As time went on, Joanne could see how her core belief that she was not enough had affected practically every area of her life. She realised that part of her desire to have a daughter came from her wish to give her husband a little girl that, yes, fitted in with her sense of not having given him enough in the sons she had given birth to. She began to recognise how familiar feelings of inadequacy and worthlessness were triggered by her underlying belief of not being enough on her own. She understood why she had never accepted an invitation to attend a social function, such as a wedding, on her own and wondered at times how her life would have been if she had accepted and had appreciated herself for being enough.

In the tradition of fairy tales, Joanne's reaching that place of acceptance could well lead to the 'happy ever after' ending in the form of a new baby girl. It could also lead to her having a deep sense of peace and contentment with not having a baby girl. Either of these could happen as Joanne relaxes and realises that she doesn't *need* to have a baby girl to make her feel complete and enough. The nagging sense of urgency, of needing to have a daughter to make her feel 'enough', disappeared the moment she became aware of it. She experienced a deep sense of peace and compassion towards herself for having wanted a girl, and knew that if she didn't she wouldn't spend the rest of her life torturing herself. What a huge gift that was to her, as well as to her family and friends!

We all have core beliefs driving us to react to situations in a particular way. Sometimes, like Joanne, we can become aware of them in a moment that transforms us for ever. I had such a moment when I became aware of my belief that I was a nuisance. Sometimes, though, knowing that a core belief is there may not be enough to stop it from causing distress.

Remember Stephen, who had the heart transplant? He discovered that knowing what he believed was not enough to make him feel better. Two thoughts that caused him particular distress were 'I'm causing everyone so much worry' and 'I hate feeling this bad.' He used the Downward Arrow technique to discover what his underlying core beliefs were and was surprised to find out that he actually had only one core belief, which was extremely powerful.

Have a look at Stephen's thought process, which is presented in fig. 5.4, noticing your own thoughts as you read his.

Fig. 5.4: Stephen's process in discovering his core belief

I'm causing every-one so much worry.		I hate feeling this bad.
↓	What's so bad about that?	↓
It's not fair on them.		I'm upsetting everyone else.
↓	What's so bad about that?	↓
It's my fault.		It's my fault.

Stephen smiled as he shrugged and said, 'You know, things generally are my fault!' When I asked him to tell me a little more about what he meant, he said, 'Well, when I was little my parents had to spend a lot of money on medication for me. That wasn't fair on everyone else, as we weren't able to go on holidays.' He had many examples to illustrate why everything, absolutely everything, that had happened in his family as he grew up was his fault. He looked at me with surprise when I asked him why. It was clear that he had never questioned his belief that everything was his fault.

While challenging core beliefs can be very effective, this is not always so. Sometimes the more a person's core beliefs are challenged the more resistant they can become. Stephen was keen to explain to me that the stress caused by his heart problems caused difficulties in his parents' relationship and was the cause of their marriage ending when he was fifteen. His sister always wanted to go to university and study medicine but was not able to do so because there was not enough money to spare.

I listened as Stephen urgently gave me example after example. A relationship he had had with a woman he really cared for when he was twenty-three did not progress, because of his heart problems. If he had been fully healthy, he told me, he could have married her and now have three children.

People who know me will have heard me say, 'Reassurance doesn't work.' Jane Austen knew how difficult persuasion could be too! I knew it would be a complete waste of time and energy to try to persuade Stephen that any of those things were not his fault. He believed they were, and anything I could say to the contrary would actually be twisted to reinforce the belief that he was right and I was wrong.

Core beliefs can be very powerful and can actually be dangerous if they are unquestioned and unchallenged. One of the best examples I know of how tragic the consequences of a core belief can be is the *Titanic* disaster. Why was it that some people had to die in that disaster? You might think it was because they hit an iceberg, because the water was cold, or even because they couldn't swim. The real reason, though, is that people believed the *Titanic* was unsinkable. There were deliberately not enough lifeboats on board; the ship was deliberately going very fast through dangerous waters; people on another ship didn't immediately respond to the distress signals; and apparently there were people on deck who refused to go into the lifeboats when disaster struck. Why? Because everyone believed that the *Titanic* would never sink. As we know, they were wrong.

So, instead of spending a lot of time and energy attempting to convince Stephen that all the things that happened in his family were his fault, we can go back to that very special and powerful word 'maybe'.

Maybe the fact that Stephen had a heart problem was not actually his fault. Maybe his parents would have separated anyway. Maybe the young woman who ended her relationship with him simply preferred to be with someone else; maybe they were just not right for each other anyway. Maybe his sister didn't have the particular abilities needed for studying medicine; maybe she wouldn't have been happy as a doctor anyway. Maybe it makes sense that people would be concerned about his health. Maybe it makes sense that he didn't feel good when he had his heart transplant.

As I showed Stephen how he could gently question his belief himself, he looked at me in amazement. 'You know,' he said, 'I have never, ever questioned that things were not my fault. I've always thought that if I were completely healthy my life would have been much better, my parents would be together, my sister would be a doctor, and everyone would be so much happier.'

Stephen smiled as I gently suggested that maybe, just maybe, he was not responsible for everyone else's happiness or un-happiness. Maybe it was all right for the people who loved him to be concerned about him. Maybe, just maybe, every single thing that happened in the entire world was not his fault! He recognised also that for him to begin to feel better he needed to act in a helpful way!

Chapter 6
Do something to feel better!

Do more than belong: participate.
Do more than care: help.
Do more than believe: practise.
Do more than be fair: be kind.
Do more than forgive: forget.
Do more than dream: work.

—WILLIAM ARTHUR WARD

Too many people wait to feel better before they do things. One of my favourite books when I was a child was *What Katy Did* by Susan Coolidge. Katy is confined to bed for some time as a result of an accident. (I hope I don't spoil the story for anyone who would like to read it.) She feels sorry for herself, becomes resentful, and is not particularly welcoming to anyone who wants to visit her. But she discovers that when she does things, even if she doesn't feel like doing them, her life is turned around for the better.

Heidi discovers the same in the book by Johanna Spyri. She feels lonely when taken from her grandfather and her friend Peter to be a companion to Clara. When she begins to make friends with Clara and make the most of her time there she starts to feel better. In *The Secret Garden* by Frances Hodgson Burnett, Mary actively persuades another Peter to begin living rather than feeling sorry for himself.

What is childhood like now for a lot of children? Those who

live in the West have grown up with rapid advances in technology. While there are undoubtedly many advantages in this, we may underestimate, or even not know, the pressures and dangers such easy access to anonymous 'friends' can cause. We have all heard reports of children and young adolescents who were groomed by someone who turns out not to be one of their own age but instead is a calculating, manipulative and controlling paedophile. 'Don't talk to strangers' was one of the protective rules I grew up with. How could it possibly apply now when so many 'friends' on the internet are actually strangers?

We can't go backwards with technology, nor would we want to; instead, it's important that we all identify and recognise certain actions as 'helpful' and others as 'unhelpful'.

The fourth question of step 2 of the Coping Triangle is 'Are your actions helpful or unhelpful'? Sometimes this may be an easy question to answer, but actions that we assume are helpful may not be. 'Talking things over' is a great example of an action that is generally assumed to be helpful but in my experience can be extremely unhelpful. It depends on the quality of the conversation. Women can talk about something for a considerable time, while men often prefer to move quickly to finding a solution for a particular problem.

Have you ever had the experience of talking about something personal only to regret it afterwards and think that you would have been better off saying nothing? I know that I have. Let's explore this using the Coping Triangle.

The situation is that I have just spent fifteen minutes discussing with a good friend something that's bothering me. Her phone rings and she immediately turns and answers it. I feel dismissed, upset and annoyed with myself. I think, *I must have been boring her, I shouldn't keep talking about myself, I'm selfish to expect her to listen to me.* I then feel embarrassed and ashamed as I think, *There I go again, talking about myself.* Lastly, I feel really annoyed with myself as I think, *I hate the way I mono-polise conversations like this. I'll never do this again.*

Fig. 6.1 shows the first step of the Coping Triangle, which is to catch the thoughts, feelings and actions I had in response to my friend answering her phone.

Fig. 6.1: *Step 1 of my Coping Triangle in response to my friend answering her phone*

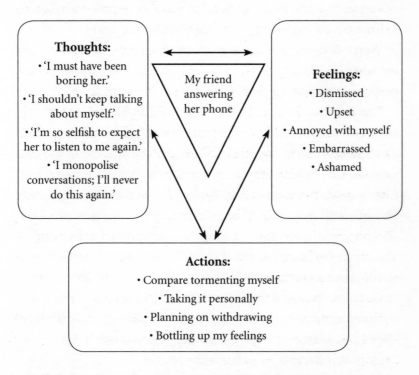

Now that I'm so used to the Coping Triangle model I often do it in my head, so that when I do write down my thoughts, feelings and actions and look at them I'm surprised by how harsh I can still be towards myself. These days, however, I tend to catch myself and recognise what's happening. Once I write my thoughts, feelings and actions down on paper I quickly go through the four questions of step 2 of the Coping Triangle.

- Do my feelings make sense?
- Are my thoughts helpful or unhelpful?
- What do I believe?
- Are my actions helpful or unhelpful?

I've had a good bit of practice doing this, so now I tend to recognise quite quickly that my feelings do make sense, given the context of what I'm thinking or what I'm doing. In this example, for instance, if the thought *I must be boring her* led me to feel wonderful we might begin to worry about me! Perhaps you'll agree with me that each of my thoughts is unhelpful. Many of them are assumptions, others are judgemental, and not one of them makes me feel good.

What might my core belief be that drives my reaction to my friend's behaviour? It will most probably be different from yours, and could be based on experiences from so long ago that I don't even remember them. I might believe that my friend didn't really want to spend time with me anyway. You may (having read this book!) probe gently and ask, 'What would be so bad about her not wanting to spend time with you?' A typical immediate response would be 'Nothing,' followed by an immediate action of tormenting myself even more for 'being so stupid and making such a big thing out of nothing.'

How could we be surprised that I would then feel worse about myself? If I was honest, though, and spent a few moments reflecting on what really would be so bad about my friend not wanting to spend time with me, I might realise that an underlying core belief such as 'I'm not enough' is behind my reaction. This could be followed by the realisation that a more fundamental core belief, that I'm stupid, is being activated—stupid to react so quickly, stupid not to read the signals that she was bored, and stupid not to have ended the conversation before she needed to give such a direct hint.

Can you see at this point how I'm taking everything so personally and how I'm exaggerating what happened? I'm probably comparing how I reacted with how more 'normal, patient, understanding' people would react. I'm also 'putting myself down.' The action I'm indulging in most is what I call 'beating myself up.' I used to do this so often that I never even realised I was doing it. The question 'Are my actions helpful or unhelpful?' has been a huge gift in helping me to see more clearly how I act and how my actions affect me as well as others around me.

My reaction to my friend answering her phone is so extreme that it's clear that it's not about her answering her phone: instead it's about what her answering her phone means to me. Without even realising it, I automatically assumed that she answered it because I was boring, and so I took everything personally. Was that a helpful action? No.

I then began to 'beat myself up' for being boring and then for being so stupid as to take this all so personally. Was that a helpful action? No.

I bottled up my feelings. This is an interesting action to reflect on. We all bottle up our feelings at times, and so long as we know that we're doing it and that it's a short-term, temporary thing I think it can be helpful. The difficulties arise when we bottle up our feelings automatically and don't realise that they're even there. We leave ourselves open to the risk that they will spill out at the worst possible times, or of denying them so severely that they resort to making us sick in order to be acknowledged.

What other actions have I been doing in my response to my friend's behaviour? Withdrawing. Withdrawing has come to be recognised as one of the warning signs that someone may be struggling to cope. Dr Coralie Wilson in Australia has done a lot of research on this. A helpful action for all of us would be to realise just how unhelpful withdrawing from others can actually be.

Most of us make comparisons so quickly that we don't even realise that we're doing it. Is comparing a helpful action? That depends really on what we're comparing and how we do it. If I realised that by comparing myself with others I had over-reacted, and if I did this in a way that was gentle, kind and compassionate towards myself, that action would have been helpful. If, however, my comparisons led me to being even more harsh and critical of myself, this action probably would not have been helpful.

Let's look a little closer at why the action of attacking ourselves can be so unhelpful. Imagine you have a little three-year-old child who spends some time with you. She might be your own daughter, a niece, a friend's child, or a grandchild. Choose someone you know if at all possible. Now picture a friend of yours saying, 'Oh, you're so lucky to be able to spend time today with that gorgeous child.' Keep picturing the child as you turn to your friend and in a sarcastic voice say, 'I get so tired being stuck with this child. You may think she's lovely, but you don't see how messy she is, how she's not able to tie her own shoelaces and how she dribbles food when she's eating.'

What would you expect the little girl to do as she listens to you? Few of us would be surprised if she began to cry, believing there was something inherently wrong about her. When we put ourselves down in this way it's as if we're attacking a three-year-old child. This is cruel and unfair. Putting ourselves down may actually make us feel better, as somehow we might think that if we suffer we're paying penance for having done something wrong. Perhaps this might be the case with people who have committed serious crimes. Just think, however, about how often you may treat yourself harshly when the 'crime' was not a crime at all. The direction to 'treat your neighbour as yourself' is very worrying if we treat ourselves badly as a matter of course!

Let's think about how Stephen and Joanne acted. Stephen was not prepared for his feelings of distress following his coronary surgery, while Joanne felt terrible that she was not able to have a daughter. Stephen concentrated on his feeling of distress and compared how he felt with how he used to feel before his surgery; he also compared how he felt with how he had expected to feel after his surgery. He told other people how he felt and blamed himself and others because he didn't feel better. He 'replayed' times when he felt better and anticipated feeling even worse.

Joanne constantly questioned herself and others about why she didn't feel happy. She tormented herself for not feeling content with her situation. She watched 'scary films' of her husband and her sons becoming tired of her and abandoning her. She switched at times into 'counting her blessings' and did her best to convince herself that she was actually fine. She compared herself with how she would like to be, isolated herself or pretended that she felt great. She also became aware that she was in fact taking help.

Table 6.1 shows each of Stephen's and Joanne's actions. If you consider any of them to be helpful, put the letter H beside them, and put a U beside those actions you consider unhelpful. I have already done this exercise, and table 6.2 shows my responses.

Are you surprised at how I have classified any of Stephen's or Joanne's actions? Sometimes it can be easy to decide whether a particular action is helpful or unhelpful; sometimes, though, it can be quite difficult and can depend on the particular context. A good example of this is Stephen telling people how he feels. The research on coping with stress emphasises social support as one of the most important coping resources we can use. This includes talking to someone else about what's really going on for us.

Table 6.1: Are Stephen's and Joanne's actions helpful or unhelpful?

Stephen's actions	Helpful or unhelpful?	Joanne's actions	Helpful or unhelpful?
Concentrate on my feelings of distress.		Question why I don't feel happy.	
Compare how I feel with how I used to feel and how I expected to feel.		Torment myself.	
Tell others how I feel.		Watch 'scary films' of my husband and sons becoming tired of me and abandoning me.	
Blame myself and others because I don't feel better.		Count my blessings.	
Replay times when I felt better.		Compare myself with how I would like to be.	
Anticipate feeling even worse.		Isolate myself or pretend.	
		Take help.	

Table 6.2: Claire's views on whether Stephen's and Joanne's actions are helpful or unhelpful

Stephen's actions	Helpful or unhelpful?	Joanne's actions	Helpful or unhelpful?
Concentrate on my feelings of distress.	U	Question why I don't feel happy.	U
Compare how I feel with how I used to feel and how I expected to feel.	U	Torment myself.	U
Tell others how I feel.	H / U	Watch 'scary films' of my husband and sons becoming tired of me and abandoning me.	U
Blame myself and others because I don't feel better.	U	Count my blessings.	H / U
Replay times when I felt better.	U	Compare myself with how I would like to be.	U
Anticipate feeling even worse.	U	Isolate myself or pretend.	U
		Take help.	H

I have always put a question mark on this action. If Stephen's conversations with his family and friends are always focused on how awful he feels, 'talking about things' can actually make him feel worse. The conversation can drag him down and make him think, 'What's the point of talking about this any more? It's not helping, and I'm only upsetting everyone else.' He might feel hopeless and could then decide not to talk to anyone again about it. He might begin to bottle up how he feels and pretend that he's grand.

You might guess that I would suggest that 'bottling up things' is not generally a helpful action. However, many of us do bottle things up at times, and as long as we know that we're doing it, and that this is a short-term action, it might be all right. An example of this would be if you're visiting someone in hospital and you discover that they look more unwell than you expected. You might feel shocked, upset and worried, but your immediate action might be to decide not to let your friend know how you feel. (Chapter 7 pulls all this together and gives some suggestions for how to deal with situations like this.)

How did you classify Joanne's action of 'counting her bless-ings'? I see it as being either helpful or unhelpful, depending on how she does it and what the outcome is for her. For instance, if she harshly berates herself for wanting a baby girl and sharply reminds herself 'just how lucky she is' to have two healthy sons, the chances are that she is going to feel worse. She is now deliberately negating something that is important to her and blaming herself for wanting it in the first place.

Sometimes it can be helpful for us to 'count our blessings' and to notice in particular the blessings that we are not usually aware of. However, Joanne will be able to really count her blessings only if she first acknowledges the hurt and upset she feels. (We'll come back to see how successfully she does this in the next chapter.)

We are often encouraged to *go* for help to someone who is considered to *give* help. Sometimes the 'help' may not be what we instinctively know is right for us. Sometimes it can actually reinforce a sense of helplessness and even dependency, so it is important to stand back and consider carefully the help that is offered and decide if we want to take it. I deliberately use the word 'take' rather than 'accept' as I see 'take' as being more proactive. Joanne was actively working with me and recognised that she was very clearly 'taking help', which she described as helpful.

Some actions are obviously unhelpful; others can become unhelpful as a result of how long we spend performing them. For instance, eating is obviously very important, and so it can be very helpful. But if we're deciding whether or not eating something is a helpful action we must consider what we eat, how we eat, how much we eat, when we eat, and even why we eat. Many activities that are usually seen to be helpful can become addictive without our realising it until it's really difficult to change things. These include such obvious things as drinking alcohol but can also include things that we might not realise are addictions, such as checking our phone for text or e-mail messages and even exercising. The old adage 'All things in moderation' is very true when we're deciding whether our actions are helpful or unhelpful.

I find that one of the most common unhelpful actions people with anxiety have is avoiding whatever it is that triggers their anxiety. While this can result in an immediate sense of relief, it's particularly unhelpful in that it reinforces the idea that the trigger causes anxiety. So, guess what happens the next time they even think about getting into a lift, going on a plane or even going down to the local shops? Yes, it's very likely that they'll feel even worse. If they decide to avoid that situation again they are at risk of setting up a vicious circle.

So what is the solution? It is, to quote the late Susan Jeffers, 'Feel the fear and do it anyway.' The essential thing is to 'do it anyway' with self-compassion. Professor Paul Gilbert has done wonderful work in demonstrating the importance of self-compassion. You can watch one of his lectures at www.youtube.com.

Let's look at some actions now that are being considered by many people to be helpful. The first one that comes to my mind is 'mindfulness'. Mindfulness courses are springing up everywhere, and there's a body of research to say that it's an effective practice in helping people cope with a range of challenges. I have met people, though, who told me that 'they tried mindfulness and it didn't work.' When I talk to them a little about what they mean it usually turns out that they tried it in order to feel happier, and because they didn't they decided it wasn't for them. I participated in an eight-week course on 'Mindfulness-Based Stress Reduction', which was developed by Jon Kabat-Zinn and taught by a wonderful teacher. You can watch a video made by Kabat-Zinn and his colleagues at the Center for Mindfulness in Medicine, Health Care and Society at the University of Massachusetts Medical School.

If I practise living mindfully, staying in the moment and meditating every single day for at least forty minutes a day, I will still have moments when I feel upset, distressed, frightened, sad, anxious or angry. Actually the more I practise mindfulness the more intensely I might feel any or all of these emotions. That can be frightening if I'm not prepared for this and blame myself for 'not doing it properly'. Mindfulness is not a tool for getting rid of feelings of distress but instead is a way of life for helping us stay with those feelings, rather than avoiding them.

There are many wonderful teachers of mindfulness. Three of my favourites are Sister Stanislaus Kennedy, Thich Nhat Hanh and Pema Chödrön, all of whom have written beautiful books.

An interview is available on line in which Thich Nhat Hanh is interviewed by Oprah Winfrey. There are many CDs on mindfulness; one I particularly like is *Moving into Stillness: Meditations from the Sanctuary* (2012) with Dr Tony Bates and Sister Stanislaus.

For centuries people of all religions have prayed in need and in gratitude. Interestingly, attention is now turning to looking at how prayer can be a helpful activity. Father Malachy Hanratty is a Columban priest who has written a beautiful book called *Discoveries in Prayer* (2007), which describes how to acknowledge and appreciate the 'good things' in life. While many people have difficulties with organised religions, the simple truth of 'love your neighbour as yourself,' which is at the heart of many religions, cannot be argued with. There is now an increased acknowledgement of the benefits of a spiritual approach to life. The truth of 'Give and you will receive' has been experienced by many people who generously volunteer their time and talents, who often describe receiving much more than they give.

It's important, of course, to recognise the truth in another saying, 'We can only give what we have,' so one of the most helpful actions any one of us can do is to recognise when our resources are so limited that we need to give priority to taking care of ourselves. This action can quickly be dismissed as 'selfish', and Carmen Renee Berry has written a wonderful book, *When Helping You Is Hurting Me: Escaping the Messiah Trap* (2003), that shows how being a 'helping messiah' doesn't help anyone and can actually hurt the people we're trying to help. Some years ago I wrote a review of the first edition of this book, called 'Hope for the "helping messiah"' (*Journal of the Institute of Guidance Counsellors*, vol. 24, 2000).

Walk into any bookshop and you'll see a vast array of 'self-help' books. I wonder sometimes whether these really do help or whether they could instead feed into an underlying core belief of 'not being good enough.' Most of them make suggestions for helpful actions, but unfortunately reading them will generally not make much difference unless we actually do some of the suggested actions! It can be very difficult to recommend one of these books, as there are so many, and what works for one person at a particular time may not work for another. Two books I often recommend are *The Dance of Intimacy* (1997) by Dr Harriet Lerner and *A Woman in Your Own Right* (1992) by Anne Dickson. While both may seem as if they are written only for women, I have found that they can be just as helpful for men.

There are lots of other actions that are helpful. Yoga, Pilates and tai-chi are all wonderful in helping us to connect with ourselves if we do them regularly. Swimming, walking, running, cycling and playing golf, tennis or any other sport can have a marvellous effect in increasing our physical fitness and our general sense of well-being. Whether they are helpful activities or not depends on how often and at what level of intensity we do them. Unfortunately, we can definitely have too much of a good thing: over-exercising can be as unhelpful as any of the other actions we can overdo, such as eating, drinking, or sleeping!

We often find it easier to identify actions that we don't like. These could be things that we do ourselves as well as things that other people do. It can be much more difficult to identify helpful actions, and we may need to ask ourselves regularly, 'What did I do well today?' and to acknowledge ourselves for that!

The next chapter shows how we can acknowledge our feelings, link them to something that makes sense and concentrate on choosing to act in a helpful way.

Chapter 7

Let's welcome it all: the good, the bad and the wonderful!

If dandelions were hard to grow, they would be most welcome on any lawn.

—ANDREW V. MASON

S o what is the Welcoming Approach again? It invites us to welcome our feelings of distress and to use the Coping Triangle three-step structured process as a way of coping with these. The first step of the Coping Triangle is to become aware of what we're thinking, how we're feeling and what we're doing about whatever it is that is causing us distress. It's important to remember that doing this may actually make us feel worse rather than better. We may feel overwhelmed, frustrated or annoyed at seeing what has been going on for us written so clearly on paper.

Don't be surprised if you don't feel any different, particularly if you're thinking such thoughts as *I don't know why I'm bothering to do this triangle, it's not going to make any difference.* Many people, myself included, find it extremely useful to do this first step. It can really help to clarify what's going on. If you do it regularly you'll begin to recognise patterns as you capture the same thoughts over and over again.

The second step of the Coping Triangle is to ask yourself the following four questions:

1. Do my feelings make sense?
2. Are my thoughts helpful or unhelpful?
3. What do I believe?
4. Are my actions helpful or unhelpful?

We've looked at how these questions relate to Stephen, who is feeling distressed at not feeling better after his heart transplant, and to Joanne, who is feeling distressed about not being able to have a daughter. Step 2 can often help people to feel better, but on its own it's not enough.

The third step is the most important. It offers a huge *céad míle fáilte* to our feelings, welcomes them as messengers that are letting us know that things are not right and recognising that we now have an opportunity to do something helpful. Think of yourself snoozing in a chair with a book by your side. You don't notice that an electric heater is faulty and is beginning to smoke. You don't notice that you're in danger. Then a brave, determined little boy tugs and pulls at you to wake you up. He might slap you, and he might even throw some water over you to wake you up. Your immediate reaction as you wake up might be to feel annoyed, and you might snap sharply at the child before trying to go back to sleep. If, however, you notice fumes and realise the danger, you're likely to act quickly to get the child and yourself to a safe place.

Just think of how grateful you would be to that little boy! He would be treated like a hero and might even be nominated for a 'Brave Child of the Year' award.

Contrast how any of us would respond to a real three-year-old child alerting us to the fact that all is not well with how we respond to our feelings of distress. Few of us welcome or thank them for giving us the opportunity to wake up and change things for the better. What would it be like if we did? I am a 'work in progress' in this regard and can vouch for how much

easier life is when I stop myself from blaming myself for how I feel and instead remind myself to welcome those feelings so that I can listen to them, learn from them and act on them. To help me do this I use what I have called the 'Coping Sentence': •
'I feel . . . because . . . (I think) . . . but . . .'

This sentence is very simple, and it's also very powerful. It provides me with an opportunity first of all to recognise and acknowledge how I feel, placing it in a context that makes sense, before looking deliberately at what I choose to do to improve my situation.

Let's see how the Coping Sentence can be used to help Stephen and Joanne. We know that their feelings make sense. Many if not all of their thoughts are unhelpful. What they believe is not true. Some of their actions are unhelpful, while some are definitely helpful. Let's build on this to consider the third step of the Welcoming Approach.

Stephen has spent hours telling himself to pull himself together, to stop being so ridiculous and to count his blessings. None of this has worked, and he's now feeling even more useless and demoralised. Let's see how the Coping Sentence can offer him a real way of welcoming, recognising and acknowledging what's going on for him and doing something concrete to improve his situation.

I feel annoyed, frustrated and completely fed up with myself, because I think I should be feeling much better, and that I'm pathetic and causing so many people distress, *but* . . .

Let's interrupt the Coping Sentence so that I can explain a little more about it. The first part, 'I feel . . .' allows Stephen to acknowledge exactly how he feels. His feelings make sense, whether in regard to what's going on for him externally or what he's thinking and believing. If Stephen is thinking that he's causing many people distress and at the same time feels wonderful we might worry. We could recognise that his thoughts are clearly unhelpful, and Stephen might recognise this too. That's why I suggest that we put the two words 'I think' after 'because'. We tend to say to ourselves, and to others, such things as 'I feel awful because it's raining' or 'I feel terrible because I let everyone down.' If instead we learn to catch what we actually think we'll perhaps realise that 'We feel awful because we think the rain is going to spoil our day,' or 'We feel terrible because we think we let everyone down.'

Do you see the difference? Even if it's actually true that I've let everyone down, putting this into the context of a thought makes it much easier for me to do something about it. And remember, just because I think it doesn't mean it's true. When I stop to think about it, how could I possibly think that I have the power to affect every single person in the world, and to have let them all down?

But, you might say, that's not what I meant. Perhaps not, but our feelings tend to take what we say literally, and if I think I've let everyone down then I will most probably feel responsible, ashamed and embarrassed. It comes back to the meaning for me of thinking that I've let everyone down, which in my case would probably be fed by my core belief of 'not having done enough.'

This is where core beliefs come in. So what might Stephen believe? If we were to explore with him what is so bad about causing people distress he might respond by saying that there's nothing bad about that really. We're not going to let him off with this, though, as clearly for him there's something really bad when he feels so awful. 'So, Stephen,' we might ask, 'let's suppose that you're right and that you should be feeling much better, and that you're pathetic, and that you're causing people a lot of distress; what's so bad about all that?' Stephen at that point might look somewhat surprised, as he may be so used to berating himself for how he feels that he has never stood back to consider what this is all about. If he accepts this question, and the following question, 'What's so bad about that?' and even another few follow-up questions, 'And what's so bad about that?' he will unearth a core belief that has been driving him to feel so bad. He might discover that he believes, really believes, that he has no right to feel distressed, has no right to look for attention and has no right to cause a fuss. He might then wonder about where this belief that 'he has no right' has come from. Now that he has brought it to light he can gently clean it off, look at it, learn from it, and even challenge it.

If you tend to perceive things visually you might relate to the idea of a core belief as something encrusted with shells being pulled from the depths of the sea, where it may have been hidden in a shipwreck. Few of us have seen exactly where the most beautiful pearls in the world come from, but we know that when they surface from water they are encased and protected in a hard exterior. Uncovering core beliefs is a very precious business, because now we can do something to gently and firmly challenge them.

As we saw in chapter 6, Stephen might believe that the fact that he is not feeling better is his fault, simply because he believes deep down that everything is his fault. He may also believe that he has no right to complain, that he has no right to feel bad. This all might be true, but it might not be. As we have seen, the more we attempt to convince Stephen that he's 'wrong' the more likely it is that his core belief will be even more firmly entrenched. So let's use the Coping Sentence as a powerful tool for helping him (*a*) to acknowledge his feelings and realise that they do make sense in relation to what he is thinking and believing and (*b*) to focus very deliberately on the helpful action he chooses to undertake.

I feel annoyed, frustrated and completely fed up with myself because I think I should be feeling much better, and that I'm pathetic and cause so many people such distress, *but maybe I'm actually doing really great to be as well as I am.*

What comes after 'but' has to be true. If Stephen used 'but I'm doing really great,' my guess is that he would immediately think, 'But that's not good enough,' which would probably cause him to feel bad again.

As I have mentioned earlier, the word 'maybe' is one of the most magical words I know. Stephen, from habit, could say, 'But maybe I'm not good enough,' but he can learn to immediately reply with 'But maybe I am!' The 'maybe' allows him to have hope rather than to sink into believing that he is definitely not good enough.

Remember that Stephen believes that the fact that he's not feeling better is his fault, because, after all, he believes that everything is his fault. All our attempts to convince him otherwise will probably end up only with him being even more convinced that everything is his fault, as he's likely to take responsibility for how we feel too.

What do you think about this suggestion?

I feel annoyed, frustrated and completely fed up with myself because I think I should be feeling much better, and that I'm pathetic and cause people so much distress, *but maybe I'm actually doing the very best I can.*

This could be effective in stopping Stephen in his 'beating himself up' pattern and in giving him an opportunity to make peace with himself, however he feels.

'Hmmm,' you may be thinking. 'But what about that selfish, self-centred woman Joanne, who's not able to recognise how lucky she is to have two healthy boys and who's making a huge fuss because she wants a baby girl too?' Of course if you are someone who relates to Joanne's distress you may have a different thought, such as 'Hmmm, but how can that help that poor woman Joanne, who is doing her best to count her blessings but who is still feeling desperately unhappy because she doesn't have the daughter she always dreamed of having?'

Do you remember that Joanne believes she has no right to want anything for herself and so is much more critical of herself for not feeling happy with her lot than anyone else could possibly be? So reminding her to 'count her blessings, pull herself together, or just get on with life,' is not going to work. Instead, let's see if one of the following Coping Sentences might help her.

— I feel furious with myself because I think I'm pathetic to want a daughter, *but I choose to learn to be kind and gentle towards the part of me that wants exactly that.*
— I feel upset because I think I'm being disloyal to the boys I have, *but my love for them is more than my feelings of upset.*
— I feel sad because I think that I do want a baby girl so much, *but that's all right.*

Notice whether you have any reaction to my suggestions. You might wonder how on earth 'but that's all right' could possibly help Joanne. If she thinks she wants a baby girl so much, it makes sense that she feels sad, and so reminding herself that her feeling of sadness is all right can be a real relief to her.

There is no one ending to the Coping Sentence that suits everyone in every situation. There are two, though, that can be useful in a wide range of situations. The first is 'I feel . . . because (I think) . . . but I will cope.' While we may worry about how we'll cope if something we don't want to happen does occur, human nature is so strong that we all tend to cope in a way that we might not have believed we were capable of.

The second is 'I feel . . . because (I think) . . . but I choose to breathe slowly.' This can be very useful, for two reasons. Firstly, the act of thinking *I choose to breathe slowly* can actually slow our breathing down, which can help us feel a little less anxious. The second is that if we concentrate on thinking *But I choose to breathe slowly* we distract ourselves from other, more unhelpful thoughts, such as *I can't . . . I don't want to . . . I'm not able to . . .* which can all cause us to feel anxiety.

I love the three steps of the Coping Triangle because they work for me and because I have seen how they have worked for so many other people. Not only am I listening to myself but I actively practise catching what I think, how I feel and what I do as the first step to coping when I feel distressed in any way. I then ask myself the four questions: 'Do my feelings make sense?' 'Are my thoughts helpful or unhelpful?' 'What do I believe?' and 'Are my actions helpful or unhelpful?' Then I spend a few moments choosing the Coping Sentence that works best for me in helping me to acknowledge my feelings of distress, to link them to something that makes sense and move then to what I choose to do to feel better.

The second part of this book deals with how we can use the Welcoming Approach in coping with some of life's challenges. These challenges may seem familiar, because they are universal. They are pressure, rejection, loss, failure, success and change. Some of the people I describe may seem familiar to you too; though none of them are real people, the challenges they face and their way of coping can be typical of ourselves and people we know.

Part 2

Let's Welcome Life's Challenges

Chapter 8
Pressure

*When we long for life without difficulties, remind
us that oaks grow strong in contrary winds and
diamonds are made under pressure.*

—PETER MARSHALL

A man and a woman were sitting in my office for the first time. Let's call the woman Stacey and the man Mike. These are not real people but I have created a story about them to show how the Welcoming Approach can be used to help us become aware of and cope with pressure.

Stacey sat forward earnestly as she told me that I was their last hope. They had been for help before and 'it hadn't worked.' A friend of Stacey's sister had met me the previous year, and over the previous few months any time Stacey spoke to her sister the conversation always ended with the dreaded question, 'Did you make that appointment yet?'

Mike seemed fed up, and I wondered whether he had come to me under protest. My guess was that they were both there because they were told to be, and while they hoped this would be different and they would actually get something from it, neither of them really believed that their visit would be helpful.

Can you feel the pressure? Some years ago I would have immersed myself, and at times almost drowned, in pressure: pressure to convince Stacey and Mike that they were not wasting their time, that there was hope, that there was help, and that I could help. Now I slow down and pay attention to the pressure itself. What is it about? Where is it coming from?

What purpose is it serving? Are there times when the pressure seems less, or even *is* less? Does everyone experience the pressure in the same way? Who is experiencing it most? Is it possible for it to be eased? What would life be like without that pressure?

What would life be like without pressure? I have no idea. Our lives are often driven by pressure, from birth to death. While it's easy enough to recognise that other people can put us under pressure, many of our own thoughts do the same.

Table 8.1 shows some of the stages in some people's lives and the 'pressure thoughts' that may accompany them. As you read them, put a tick beside any that directly relate to you. There is also space for you to write in any additional pressure thoughts that you have had if you have experienced some of these particular life pressures.

Table 8.1: Some life stages and pressure thoughts

Falling in love	— What if it doesn't work out?
	— What if he / she leaves me?
	— What if I get too close to him / her and then it's over?
	— What if my family / friends don't like him / her?
	— I'm not good enough for him / her.
	— What if he / she is not good enough?
	— I don't think he / she is 'the one.'
	— Does he / she make me happy enough?
	— Can I ever make him / her happy enough?
	— We've been going out together for a while; should we move in together?
	— Should we become engaged?
	— Should we get married?

Additional pressure thoughts I have had:

—

—

—

Getting married   — Is this the right thing for me?

— How can I know that I really do want to marry him / her?

— What if it doesn't work out?

— How can we afford to get married anyway?

— We can't even agree on who to ask to the wedding.

— It's all so expensive.

— We're going to offend some of our family and friends by not asking them, but we just can't afford a big wedding.

— He / she is insisting on having / not having a church wedding.

— Why should I give in to something I don't want? It's my wedding too!

— What if I get too close to him / her and then it's over?

— What if my family / friends don't like him / her?

— What if I'm not good enough?

— What if he / she is not good enough?

— What if I do or say something stupid?

— What if I change my mind at the last minute?

— It's my wedding, so it has to be perfect.

Additional pressure thoughts I have had:

—

—

—

_____

_____

Wanting to conceive —Why isn't it happening?

     — What am I doing wrong?

     — He / she needs to go to the doctor for tests.

     — What if it's me?

     — What if I can never have a child of my own?

     — I'm not going to have only one child: I have
to have another one (two, three . . .)

     — He / she just has to cut down on alcohol /
give up smoking . . .

Additional pressure thoughts I have had:

—

—

—

_____

_____

Pregnancy —What if we lose the baby?

     — What if there's something wrong with the
baby?

     — I'll be a terrible mother / father.

     — I'm probably far too young / too old to be
having this baby.

     — I wish I / she hadn't smoked / taken that
medicine / drunk so much when I / she was
first pregnant and didn't know it.

— Could I / she have harmed my baby?

— I'm never going through this again.

— I have to go through this again to have at least one more child.

— I don't think I can do it.

— I have to do it.

— This is too much.

— I'm supposed to be enjoying this special time of my life.

Additional pressure thoughts I have had:

—

—

—

_____

Right now, please stop and catch what you're thinking as you read the various pressure thoughts above. You may have identified completely with them and in fact may feel some ease in your own feeling of pressure as you realise that other people have the same types of pressure thoughts as you. You may, however, feel irritable or excluded if you're single or have no interest in having a baby. Perhaps you're someone who has spent years wanting to have a child and, for whatever reason, don't have one. If you're one of the many people who have had difficulties with relationships you may feel angry and upset. You may wonder why I didn't have 'relationship break-up' in there too.

I don't intend to cause you any upset or distress, but it's likely that however you are feeling right now makes sense, according to what your particular life circumstances are or what you're thinking and what you're doing.

We all experience pressure. Table 8.2 lists a few more of life's challenges. I don't wish to put you under any pressure, but have a look at these and see if any of them relate to you.

Table 8.2: Some more life stages and pressure thoughts

Doing exams	— I hate studying.
	— I'll never get it all done.
	— I've left it too late.
	— I have to do well in this.
	— If I don't do well I'll disappoint . . .
	— It's not fair that I have to study.
	— I wish I didn't have to do this.
	— Look at . . . He or she didn't do this exam and is getting on really well anyway.
	— This is such a waste of time.

- -

Additional pressure thoughts I have had:

—

—

—

_____

_____

Working	— This isn't the job for me.
	— This isn't how I thought my life was going to be.
	— I'm not earning enough.
	— No-one really appreciates how hard I work.
	— I'm not getting paid enough.
	— I should ask for a pay increase.
	— I shouldn't have to ask for a pay increase.

— My boss doesn't seem happy with my work.

— I'm making mistakes.

— I used to be better.

— I need to work harder.

— I need to earn more.

— Should I be looking for another job?

— What if I can't find another job?

— Do I really want to move anyway?

— I'm not as happy working as I thought I would be.

— The others at work all seem more capable, more sociable or more confident than me.

— What if I leave this job and can't get another one?

— What if I leave this job and regret it?

Additional pressure thoughts I have had:

—

—

—

_____

_____

Retiring

— I don't know whether I can afford to retire.

— What will I do with my time?

— I should do some sort of course to prepare myself for retirement.

— I'm not good at golf / bridge / not working.

— How will I spend my days?

— I don't want to retire.

— I do want to retire, but I have another few years to go.

— Everyone else seems much better prepared
for retirement than me.

— I have to work harder before I retire.

— I have to use my time really well now that
I'm retired.

Additional pressure thoughts I have had:

—

—

—

_____

When we stop to think about all the different life stages we
go through we can see there is probably none that has no
pressure. We would all like to think that when we reach a
certain age we'll no longer have pressure; yet think of the
pressures many people cope with as they come into the time of
life that used to be described as old age. They are often
inspiring as they quietly cope with the pressures associated
with a range of challenges, such as loss.

While some life events, such as giving birth, doing exams
and retiring, can be wonderful experiences, it's important that
we acknowledge the pressure that can accompany them. If we
don't we may not recognise it until it has become too much
and we, or someone close to us, becomes seriously ill. Do you
remember my use of a volcano to explain how many of us lock
away feelings we don't like or don't think we should have? They
don't go away, and, left too long without attention, they can
cause all sorts of difficulties, including headaches and stomach
problems. Somehow there can be a sense of shame in
recognising that we are actually under pressure.

How would it be if we welcomed our feeling of pressure into

our lives rather than seeing it as something we should be ashamed of? Do you remember the fairy tale of Sleeping Beauty? The 'bad fairy' arrived at the baby's christening with her spiteful gift of death at the moment the child pricked her finger on a spindle. Just think of the pressure to ensure that all the spindles in the country were destroyed! However, because that pressure was recognised and acknowledged, a 'good fairy' was able to do something positive by ensuring that the child would not die but would fall asleep until she was awakened by true love's kiss.

Table 8.3 lists some of life's challenges that we all face, as well as some of the pressure thoughts that may accompany them. As you read them, become aware of your own thoughts, be gentle with how you feel and notice if you want to stop reading, or cry, or distract yourself or read on. It's very important that you are gentle with yourself. Life is pressured enough as it is!

Table 8.3: Some life stages and pressure thoughts we will all experience

Sickness	— What's wrong with me / him / her?
	— What if I don't get better?
	— What if he / she doesn't get better?
	— Could the tests be wrong?
	— I hate this.
	— This is so unfair!
	— How can I keep going with this?
	— I have to keep going.
	— I wish I had done something different earlier.
	— It's too late.
	— I'm causing so much fuss.

— This shouldn't be about me.

— I feel frightened.

— I have to show a good example.

— I have to be strong.

Additional pressure thoughts I have had:

—

—

—

Death

— I'm not ready for this.

— I don't want to face this.

— I wish I'd done things differently.

— There's so much now that needs to be done, and time is so short.

— I have to do it all.

— It's not right that I have to do it all.

— Where is everyone else?

— I wish I knew the exact moment of death.

— What happens after death?

— Is this all there is?

— What's it all about anyway?

Additional pressure thoughts I have had:

—

—

Let's turn things around and welcome the feelings and thoughts associated with pressure so that we can concentrate on how we can deliberately act in a way that will either reduce pressure or at least make sure it doesn't get out of control.

STACEY AND MIKE

Let's look at how the Welcoming Approach can help Stacey and Mike with whatever it is that's causing them pressure.

I needed to establish a trusting relationship with them both, acknowledging that Mike possibly might not want to be with me anyway. Stacey clearly was desperately worrying about what would happen when (not if!) this didn't work. So, instead of first hearing what had brought them to me, I said something like 'My sense right now, even before you tell me why you're here, is that you, Mike, are thinking, "This is not going to work," and you, Stacey, are hoping desperately that it will. I'm conscious that you've really been sent by your sister, and Mike, you look as if you might be here under protest.'

Mike shrugged his agreement. He didn't really want to be there and saw it as a waste of time. Stacey began to cry and asked him to please give this a chance. I gently asked them both if I could show them a model that I really like, as it might be of some help to them. I gave them a brief introduction to my work, explaining how I became interested in cognitive behavioural therapy (CBT). I also discussed confidentiality and the specific limits to do with abuse and the immediate risk of self-harm or of harming others. I explained that if they found this model helpful we could then use it to look at whatever it was that brought them to see me in the first place.

Stacey and Mike looked at each other, and as they both nodded for me to continue I could sense some relief. They didn't at that point need to tell me whatever had been causing them distress; instead that moment was about how the two of them were right then.

Some people would find this very difficult: they would prefer me to listen while they tell me exactly what has been going on for them, and in those instances I would listen. My instinct with Stacey and Mike, however, was that they had shared whatever was distressing them with each other, family, friends and professionals and didn't find that particularly helpful. Before they could go there again we needed to look at what was going on for them right now and welcome those feelings and thoughts.

As I drew two inverted triangles on a page I asked Stacey and Mike in turn what they were thinking, how they were feeling, and what they were doing in relation to coming to meet me. Fig. 8.1 and fig. 8.2 show their responses to this first step of the Coping Triangle.

It can be very difficult to do step 1. Stacey seemed surprised that Mike was as set against getting help as he seemed to be. She said they had been to two therapists in the previous twelve months to sort things out and Mike had never said that he wouldn't go. She hadn't realised that he was going with her each time under silent protest. Mike was very clear that step 1 was of no help to him whatsoever—in fact it confirmed for him what he had already known, only that instead of going round in circles we were just 'going round in triangles.'

Fig. 8.1: Step 1 of Stacey's Coping Triangle in response to coming for help

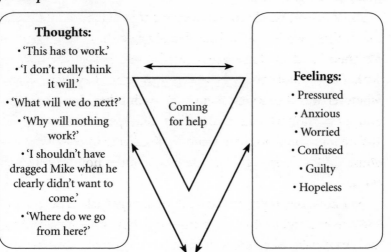

Thoughts:
- 'This has to work.'
- 'I don't really think it will.'
- 'What will we do next?'
- 'Why will nothing work?'
- 'I shouldn't have dragged Mike when he clearly didn't want to come.'
- 'Where do we go from here?'

Coming for help

Feelings:
- Pressured
- Anxious
- Worried
- Confused
- Guilty
- Hopeless

Actions:
- Doing what her sister told her to do.
- Anticipating that nothing will work to improve things.
- Worrying.
- Questioning why nothing has worked so far.
- Blaming herself for putting Mike under pressure.

Fig. 8.2: Step 2 of Mike's Coping Triangle in response to coming for help

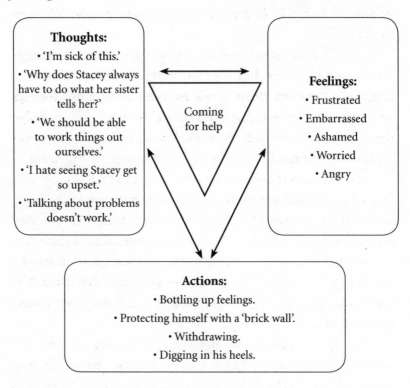

Both Stacey and Mike were willing for me to continue with the other two steps of the Coping Triangle. When I asked Stacey if her feelings made sense she immediately said, 'No, they don't, because I shouldn't be so negative.' She nodded as I suggested that she had now slipped into judging herself harshly, and Mike said, 'You do that a lot, Stacey.' Her look of surprise to him was a moment when something seemed to shift between them. They were now acknowledging what was going on for each other and communicating differently. Mike agreed that his feelings made sense but said he was tired of feeling that way. His level of frustration seemed high as he said, 'Stacey, you don't ever talk about anything else any more. All you say is that things need to change and that we need to talk to the right person for things to change. There's no right person. We need to change.'

Remember that at this point I still have no idea what changes they're talking about; but it's clear that something different is happening between them. I talk to them both about feelings being like lava in volcanoes and how if we don't acknowledge them they can burst out in an explosion, or leak out passive-aggressively, or continue buried, busily causing greater harm.

Again the two of them, who were now clearly working with me, acknowledged the pressure they were both experiencing as well as their surprise that they hadn't recognised that pressure until now. Stacey explained that she felt under massive pressure to do what her sister said and was worried about how she was going to explain to her that her idea hadn't worked. She was anticipating her sister's response that she just hadn't tried hard enough.

Mike spoke about the pressure of having to pay for something that would 'sort itself out' over time. He also described his feeling of embarrassment that Stacey was discussing their private lives with her sister, and his frustration at being unable to make Stacey happy. As this conversation was evolving I was adding to their triangles, as can be seen in fig. 8.3 and fig. 8.4.

Fig. 8.3: Stacey's amended Coping Triangle following a discussion about what it was like to do step 1

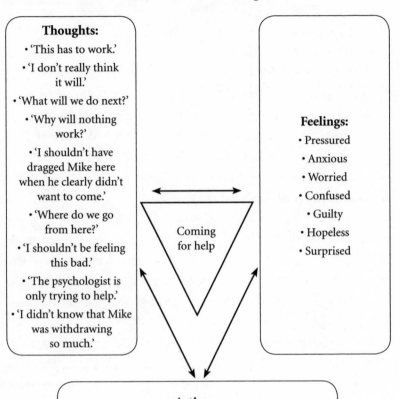

Thoughts:
- 'This has to work.'
- 'I don't really think it will.'
- 'What will we do next?'
- 'Why will nothing work?'
- 'I shouldn't have dragged Mike here when he clearly didn't want to come.'
- 'Where do we go from here?'
- 'I shouldn't be feeling this bad.'
- 'The psychologist is only trying to help.'
- 'I didn't know that Mike was withdrawing so much.'

Coming for help

Feelings:
- Pressured
- Anxious
- Worried
- Confused
- Guilty
- Hopeless
- Surprised

Actions:
- Doing what her sister told her to do.
- Anticipating that nothing will work to improve things.
- Worrying.
- Questioning why nothing has worked so far.
- Blaming herself for putting Mike under pressure.
- Judging.
- Tormenting herself.

Fig. 8.4: Mike's amended Coping Triangle following a discussion about what it was like to do step 1

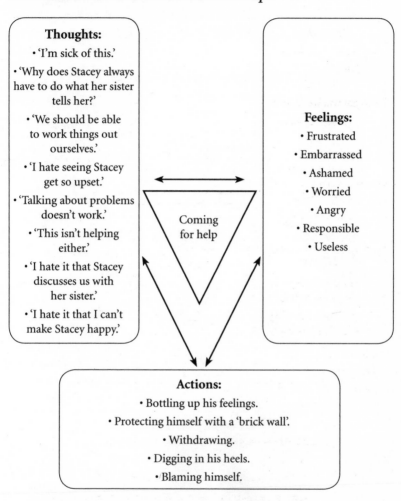

Question 2 of the second step of the Coping Triangle model is 'Are your thoughts helpful or unhelpful?' Stacey and Mike nodded in agreement as the three of us considered each thought and decided that they were all unhelpful, because they triggered such feelings as frustration and pressure. They were also unhelpful because they kept them locked into a pattern of conflict and difficult communication.

The third question is vital. What did Mike believe about coming to me for help, and what did Stacey believe? Clearly they both believed that it was not going to work, so we explored this using the Downward Spiral, as illustrated in fig. 8.5.

Fig. 8.5: Uncovering Stacey's and Mike's core beliefs

Stacey	Coming to a psychologist for help won't work.	Mike
↓	What's so bad about that?	↓
My sister will be disappointed with me.		We'll have talked about our difficulties and upset Stacey for nothing.
↓	What's so bad about that?	↓
She won't give me any more advice.		We shouldn't have to go outside the family for help.
↓	What's so bad about that?	↓
I'll have to make decisions on my own.		People who aren't family won't really care about you.
↓	What's so bad about that?	↓
I'm not able to make the right decisions.		People will let you down.

Stacey was amazed to discover a core belief she never realised she had. But it rang true for her and explained why she never trusted herself to make any important decision. However, when we questioned whether this belief was 100 per cent true 100 per cent of the time she realised immediately that it wasn't. Laughing, she said she was well able to decide what she was going to wear to work and didn't need a family conference every day to help her do it. She recognised how powerful this belief had been and described how every time something went wrong or wasn't fixed she immediately took responsibility for having made the wrong decision.

Mike was at first not sure whether or not he had a core belief that people would let him down. He did agree that when he was growing up one of his family rules was never to discuss 'family business' with anyone outside the family. He had never questioned why this might be so. Stacey listened carefully and then said, 'Mike, when we first met I remember asking you if there was something wrong, and you shut me out. It turned out that you and your brother had made a very bad investment, and you were worried about it. Do you remember how upset I was that you wouldn't confide in me? You said at the time that I wasn't family.'

Mike nodded, looking a bit embarrassed, and acknowledged that, yes, it had always been important for him that what was going on in the family should be kept within the family.

As we know, 'no matter what they tell us, what we believe is true.' So I wasn't going to spend time trying to convince Mike that it was safe to confide in me. Nor was I going to convince Stacey that she was able to make decisions for herself, irrespective of what her sister wanted her to do. I suggested instead that perhaps the pressure they had both experienced in attending me was in fact a blessing. It was showing them clearly that they weren't happy with the idea of getting help, and it was no surprise really that their previous two attempts to get help had not worked.

Question 4 of the second step of the Coping Triangle puts the focus on whether Stacey's and Mike's actions were helpful or unhelpful. They recognised that several of their actions were clearly unhelpful. However, they were clear that the fact that they were discussing, really discussing, how they genuinely felt and thought about getting help was helpful.

At this point I suggested that they were both in fact taking my help. They agreed and were keen to see what the third and final step of the model is and how they could use it to help them improve whatever was going on for them.

The Coping Sentence that Stacey liked best was:

I feel under pressure because I think that I will not make the right decision, *but I recognise and appreciate my ability to make decisions that are right for me.*

Mike could see how Stacey's Coping Sentence could make a real difference to her and wondered what would work for him. The three of us considered a number of suggestions before he nodded, saying, 'I like that. Yes, that would work for me.' His favourite Coping Sentence was:

I feel frustrated in accepting help, because I think I should be able to do things on my own, *but I choose to practise asking for and accepting help when I need it.*

While the meaning of getting help was different for Stacey and for Mike, it reinforced a sense of helplessness and inadequacy. Getting help in fact was increasing pressure between them. Until this was addressed it was going to be extremely difficult for them to take help.

You may be wondering what exactly brought Stacey and Mike for help in the first place. At this point it doesn't really matter. It could be because of difficulties connected with Mike and his sixteen-year-old daughter from a previous relationship and how they were affecting Mike and Stacey's own ten-year-old twins. Perhaps it was rooted in Stacey's concern for her older sister, who was very ill and was eating into time that was supposed to be 'family time.' Stacey made the appointment because her sister told her to, so perhaps her sister thought that coming to see me would help Stacey and Mike sort out difficulties in their own relationship.

The reasons could be many and complex. The result was that neither Stacey nor Mike was in a position to really take any sort of help, because of the pressure they were both under. Once that pressure was acknowledged and, yes, actually welcomed, they were free to begin looking at whatever else was causing them distress too.

You may have identified with either Stacey or Mike, or you may not have. While life's challenges may be similar, they can affect each of us very differently according to our own strengths, resilience, supports, and ability to take the supports available to us.

Why is it that some people cope better with pressures than others? Why is it that some people see pressures as opportunities, while others find that pressures create more pressures? The answers can often be found in what we believe about pressure in the first place. Exercise 8.1 is a simple one I've devised that can help you uncover your own beliefs about pressure. Complete it quickly without thinking about it too much.

Exercise 8.1: Uncovering beliefs about pressure

---

1. Pressure for me is

---

2. I know I'm experiencing pressure when I

---

3. When I experience pressure I

---

4. Some people recognise when I'm under pressure from

---

5. Other people don't spot when I'm under pressure because I

Pressure can be linked with probably all of life's challenges. It can result from external demands and insufficient resources. Pressure can also be caused by internal harsh, pressurising thoughts as well as from a reluctance to ask for and take support. Particular thoughts that can directly increase pressure contain such words as 'should,' 'must' and 'have to.' It can be particularly helpful, then, in acknowledging the feelings of pressure in the Coping Sentence to use the word 'choose'. Rather than blaming ourselves for experiencing pressure, let's welcome it, knowing that we experience it as a real aid to choosing to do something about things to relieve that pressure!

Chapter 9
Rejection

*I don't want to belong to any club that will accept
me as a member.*

—GROUCHO MARX

How many people do you know who do their absolute
best to fit in? We have all probably done so at some
stage in our lives. If you have an opportunity to visit a
creche you may be shocked by how direct young children can
be. If they don't want to play with another child they will
usually make that very clear. Adults tend to be on the watch to
ensure that no child is excluded. Children who prefer to play
alone can quickly be labelled as 'loners'. Their parents are often
advised to develop their children's social skills so that the
children 'fit in.' Children who really don't want someone as a
friend can wrongly be labelled as 'bullies' and told that they
have to play with everyone.

Experiences of rejection are part and parcel of life, however.
Some people are able to cope with it, while others struggle. We
even hear tragic stories of young people who are unable to
cope with such challenges as the break-up of a relationship or
being made redundant and who take their own life.

Let's do things differently. Let's welcome our experience of
rejection as one of the best learning experiences we'll ever have!

Right now, think of a time when you felt rejected. Where
were you? What age were you? Who was with you? What was it
like to feel rejected? What happened then? Now take a few
moments to complete the Rejection Exercise below.

Exercise 9.1: The Rejection Exercise

Where were you when you felt rejected?	
What age were you?	
Who rejected you?	
Why?	
What was said to you?	
Did anyone support you?	
What was it like for you to feel rejected?	
What happened then?	
What did you learn from this experience?	

What was it like for you to do that exercise? Now complete the Coping Triangle in fig. 9.1 to separate out how you're feeling, what you're thinking and what you're doing as you focus on your experience of rejection.

Fig. 9.1: My thoughts, feelings and actions as I think about my experience of rejection

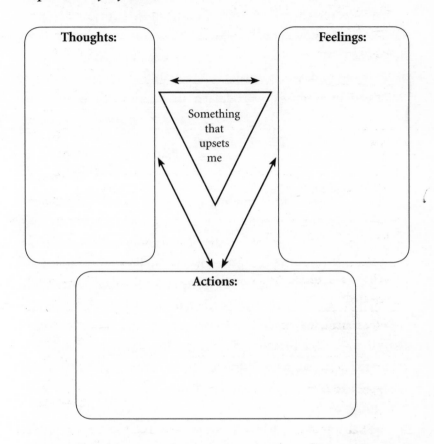

Ask yourself whether your feelings make sense; then see if your thoughts are 'helpful' or 'unhelpful'. See if you can uncover what core belief you have that's driving your reaction. Then concentrate on whether your actions are helpful or unhelpful. Finally, see if you can complete the Coping Sentence with a strong and powerful statement.

There are many ways in which any of us can experience rejection. It may well be that the person or people we think are rejecting us are not in fact doing so, but our experience will be one of rejection anyway. Sometimes because we expect people not to like us this becomes our experience.

This was the case of one girl, Sarah, whose fictitious story is summarised below. This is followed by two other stories I have devised: Andy, a 34-year-old worried Casanova, and Terry, a 48-year-old man who was angry and troubled. In each case the Rejection Exercise was particularly useful in helping them to uncover what they began to believe as a result of their experience of having been rejected.

SARAH

Sarah was fifteen and struggling to fit in with her peers when her parents came to me for help. They described her as being 'too bright for her own good.' She had recently been assessed as being in the top fifth percentile for her intellectual ability: that means that she was as bright as, or brighter than, 95 per cent of fifteen-year-olds. They explained that Sarah had always been different from her peers. She was quieter and more reserved than them. In the previous six months her parents had noticed that she had become withdrawn and no longer asked to meet friends, and they were concerned that her school work was beginning to be affected. They had made several attempts to discuss their concerns with Sarah, but each time the brief conversation ended with her bursting into tears, begging them to leave her alone.

When I met Sarah she told me that 'everything is fine' and that her parents had the problem, not her. She agreed that we could use her unhappiness with parents as a way of my explaining the Coping Triangle to her. Fig. 9.2 shows her thoughts, feelings and actions in relation to her parents.

Fig. 9.2: Sarah's Coping Triangle on what was causing her most distress

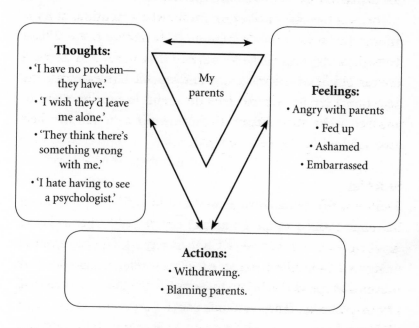

Thoughts:
- 'I have no problem—they have.'
- 'I wish they'd leave me alone.'
- 'They think there's something wrong with me.'
- 'I hate having to see a psychologist.'

My parents

Feelings:
- Angry with parents
- Fed up
- Ashamed
- Embarrassed

Actions:
- Withdrawing.
- Blaming parents.

Sarah's parents had told me that they were concerned about her eating habits. At this point she was clearly not going to discuss this with me, so I went fully with what she was willing to deal with. We went through the four questions of step 2, and I found her resistance melting a little when we were looking at question 3: 'What do you believe?' Using the Downward Arrow technique, I asked Sarah, 'What's so bad about your parents thinking that there's something wrong with you?' She looked at me somewhat bewildered and said, 'Because there isn't.'

I followed that by asking, 'So what's so bad about them thinking that there's something wrong with you when there isn't?' Sarah hesitated for a moment and then quietly said, 'Because they're right.' When I asked what she meant she looked directly at me and said, 'My parents are right. There is something wrong with me.'

Tears gently began to fall, releasing some of the pressure Sarah was carrying, as she told me about her experiences with her classmates. No matter what she did she seemed to be wrong. If she went over to one of them and said, 'Hi. I heard you talking about that new song you downloaded. Is it good?' she got a cold look and was spitefully asked, 'Why do you want to know?' If she ignored everyone and sat on her own at lunchtime she overheard nasty comments that were directed at her. She had deliberately stopped working hard in class to see if that would make a difference, but it didn't. All that happened when puzzled teachers asked her why her grades had dropped was that her classmates sniggered nastily.

When I asked Sarah if this had always been her experience with her peers she shrugged hopelessly, saying that it was. I asked her to think of one particular experience when she felt rejected by girls her age and to complete the Rejection Exercise. Table 9.1 shows Sarah's responses.

Table 9.1: Sarah's responses to the Rejection Exercise

Where were you when you felt rejected?	In the school playground.
What age were you?	Eight.
Who rejected you?	Three girls in my class.
Why?	They didn't like me.
What was said to you?	'You can't play with us.'
Did anyone support you?	No.
What was it like for you to feel rejected?	Awful, absolutely awful.

What happened then?	I pretended I didn't care.
What did you learn from this experience?	That there's something wrong with me.

Sarah was clearly committed to completing this exercise honestly. She had confided in me that her parents were right. She wasn't feeling happy.

Doing this exercise was a revelation to her. She realised that her pattern of pretending that she was fine and that she didn't care went back to a time when she was eight years old. She looked at me stunned as she said, 'But I don't even like those girls now.' She realised that she was different from them and that she really had nothing in common with them. We talked about how as an eight-year-old she had deliberately hidden her feelings of hurt and upset when she was rejected. This had become a pattern that she continued right up to the present. She was struck by how her core belief that there was something wrong with her had meant that she actually expected other people of her age not to like her. She realised that this made her feel anxious, and that this had in fact become a self-fulfilling prophecy. The more relaxed she was in herself, irrespective of whether her peers liked her, the better.

Sarah realised that just because she believed she was not popular didn't make that true. She was only fifteen, so maybe she would meet people who would become lifelong friends as she got older. She realised that deliberately doing poorly in her school work as a way of becoming popular was not helpful and was actually limiting her future opportunities. It became important for her once more to do her best, irrespective of how her classmates responded.

She began to relax about needing to be included and changed her expectation of being excluded and rejected. As a result she discovered that she actually felt happier. She began to see how she could use her feelings of upset and anxiety as indicators that she needed to relax and accept herself more. As she practised this she found that she had moments when she actually felt at peace. She found the following Coping Sentences to be particularly helpful:

— I feel upset because I think I'm not popular, *but I choose to breathe slowly.*
— I feel upset because I think I'm not popular, *but I choose to recognise and appreciate the social skills I use every day.*
— I feel upset because I think I'm not popular, *but maybe my lifelong friends are getting ready to meet me.*

ANDY

Andy was thirty-four years old. He made an appointment to see me when a previous girl-friend turned the other way on seeing him in the street. He was surprised, as he was pleased to see her, and he ran after her to see if she was all right. He was totally taken aback when she began to shout obscenities at him and said she never wanted to have anything to do with him again. Andy was stunned, as he liked this woman and was upset at the idea that he might have caused her any difficulty.

Her reaction was the catalyst for him to get help in looking at his pattern of having brief, intense relationships. He described his social life as 'wonderful if I was still twenty-two years old.' As he was getting older he realised that many of his friends had settled into long-term relationships, some were getting married, and quite a few had children. His former girl-friend's extreme reaction had made him question himself and wonder why he treated women the way he did. The first step of Andy's Coping Triangle is shown in fig. 9.3.

Fig. 9.3: Andy's Coping Triangle on what was causing him most distress

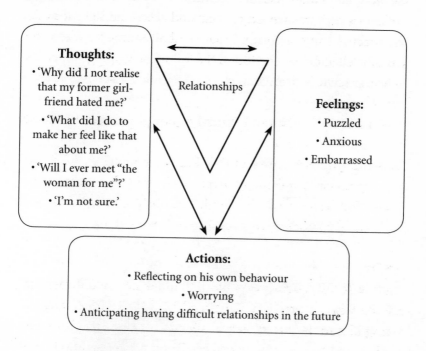

Thoughts:
• 'Why did I not realise that my former girl-friend hated me?'
• 'What did I do to make her feel like that about me?'
• 'Will I ever meet "the woman for me"?'
• 'I'm not sure.'

Relationships

Feelings:
• Puzzled
• Anxious
• Embarrassed

Actions:
• Reflecting on his own behaviour
• Worrying
• Anticipating having difficult relationships in the future

It's not surprising that step 1 of the Coping Triangle didn't make Andy feel better. He felt embarrassed enough at coming to see me in the first place. Focusing on his feelings, thoughts and actions made him feel a bit worse, as he told me: 'This is ridiculous that I'm here talking about this.' He was very open with me in reviewing his pattern of relationships over the previous ten years and was visibly shocked to realise that he had had many more girl-friends than he could remember. His longest relationship was for eighteen months, and he sheepishly told me that that ended because his girl-friend discovered that he was sleeping with two of her friends! We both agreed that this was probably not the best example of a long-term relationship in the first place!

When I asked Andy if any of his previous girl-friends had ended their relationship, he surprised himself by how forcefully he responded, 'I never gave them a chance.' I gently asked him if he could remember any experience of having been rejected by a woman, and he silently nodded.

He was willing to complete the Rejection Exercise, and his responses are given in table 9.2. As you read them, pay attention to your own thoughts and feelings.

Table 9.2: Andy's responses to the Rejection Exercise

Where were you when you felt rejected?	At home reading a text message.
What age were you?	Twenty-two.
Who rejected you?	A girl I had really liked.
Why?	I don't know.
What was said to you?	'I don't want to be with you any more.'
Did anyone support you?	Yes, my brother and my mother.
What was it like for you to feel rejected?	It was probably the most painful experience I had ever had up until then.
What happened then?	I locked myself into my room for three weeks, and then asked her friend out.
What did you learn from this experience?	That you can't trust what girls say, and that I can survive anyway.

Andy sat with his hands clenched as he told me that he hadn't allowed himself to think of that experience for years. I asked him the name of the woman, and whether he knew anything about her now. It was clearly very difficult for him to even think about her, and it took a little while for him to compose himself enough to tell me about her. Her name was Tara, and he clearly saw her as having been the love of his life. His puzzlement hadn't faded over the years as Andy told me that he still had no idea why she had ended their relationship. They had gone out for eight months, and he had been convinced that they were going to get married and live happily ever after.

I asked Andy if he had ever spoken to Tara again, and particularly if he had asked why she ended their relationship by text message. That obviously wasn't of great concern to him, as he shrugged and said, 'Text was probably easier.' He spoke to her only once since, shortly after he began going out with her best friend, and that was to tell her that he had never cared about her anyway. He began to speak very quickly as he told me that this wasn't true: he had been broken-hearted on receiving her message but was never going to tell her that.

I wondered whether Andy had spent years blaming and punishing all the women he had gone out with for Tara's rejection of him. I gently asked him this, and while he first looked surprised he then put his head in his hands and sighed deeply. He began to tell me just how awful he was to successive girlfriends. He stopped suddenly at one point. 'I've just realised,' he said in amazement, 'why my previous girl-friend ran in the opposite direction from me.'

When I asked if he would like to share that with me Andy blushed and said he was now beginning to think that the woman was right. Speaking quickly, he described telling her that he couldn't go with her to a particular concert she was looking forward to, as he was really sick and wasn't able to leave his bed. He hadn't expected her to come over to see how he was, only to discover that the reason he wasn't leaving his bed was called Isabel and had nothing to do with illness.

'That was only a few months ago,' Andy said in dismay. 'How could I possibly have forgotten that I treated her so badly?'

By now Andy was feeling ashamed, embarrassed, humiliated, upset and angry with himself. I suggested that he welcome these feelings in as messengers that were telling him that the relationship area in his life was not going very well! Andy listened carefully and asked how he could change his pattern. He realised that he really did believe that he couldn't trust his heart to a woman; in the process he had begun to behave in such a way that he couldn't be trusted.

As it's action that makes changes happen, Andy agreed with my suggestion that he deliberately take a break from relationships for at least six months. During that time he was to get to know women as people, as opposed to women who were to pay for what Tara had done to him. He decided himself that he would write to the woman he had met in the street and apologise for how he had treated her. He also wanted to thank her for running away, as that was definitely the wake-up call for him.

Andy left my office definitely feeling worse than when he came in. Now, though, he recognised that it made sense for him to feel as bad as he did. He had already changed his pattern of pretending he was fine and covering up. We discussed a number of Coping Sentences, and the one he found that applied best to him was:

I feel embarrassed because of how I treated women I've met over the past ten years, *but I choose to learn how to communicate with women honestly.*

In today's world there is a perception that young men are particularly vulnerable to taking their own life when confronted with life's challenges. While Andy recognised that his behaviour with women was not right or fair, he was a lot more resilient than he had realised. When Tara sent him that upsetting message when he was twenty-two Andy confided in his mother and brother. He found them to be very supportive, and he knew that no matter what he ever did they would support him.

Andy left my office with his phone in his hand: he was sending a text message to his mother and brother, inviting them to meet him for coffee. He wanted to thank them for being so supportive and to share with them just how deplorable his behaviour had been. He wanted to do this because he wanted to begin developing honest communication with the two people he cared most about.

Andy welcomed one of the most difficult experiences in his life as having something to teach him. He has my admiration and respect, and he proves that young men can be just as courageous, humble and resilient as men and women of any age.

He attended me for a few more sessions and found imagery and relaxation techniques to be particularly helpful in giving him hope and in helping him change his patterns in establishing and maintaining relationships. I'm hopeful that he will never again experience a previous girl-friend running in the opposite direction on seeing him.

TERRY

Terry is a 48-year-old man who was worried that everything he had worked so hard for was disappearing before his eyes. He trained as a chartered accountant and left a large practice ten years ago to work for himself. At first the change went well, as some of his former clients supported him. However, his sarcastic, cynical and disrespectful attitude to the people he met had driven many of his clients away. His wife, Nora, had become increasingly concerned at the level of his anger, which too often was directed towards her and the youngest of their three children, aged eleven. Following a row in which Nora threatened to leave him, Terry said he would get help and would change.

Terry met me with his head down. He didn't look me in the eye and looked as if he would prefer to be absolutely anywhere else. When I said this to him he nodded that I was right. I asked him what it meant for him to have a conversation with me. He told me he couldn't believe he had sunk so low; for him, having to come to see me was the ultimate proof of the failure he had become.

At this point I had no idea why he was sitting across from me, but I did know that if he believed he was a failure I wasn't going to convince him otherwise. Instead of falling into that trap I suggested that perhaps whatever brought him to see me could be a turning-point for him. He had a choice: he could make his visit to me a confirmation of how terrible he was or use it as the marker for things improving for himself and for others.

Terry shrugged and said, 'Well, I'm here now, so let's make the most of it.' He was very open with me as I asked detailed questions to get a sense of his past and his areas of strength as well as his vulnerabilities. It became apparent as we did so that his life was divided into two phases: before an e-mail message telling him he hadn't got the promotion he wanted, and after. Terry was somewhat bewildered that he had shared that experience with me, as he said that he had never told anyone about it before. Not getting the promotion was the catalyst for him leaving to work for himself, as he told me he could never again work for people who undervalued him so much.

At this point I asked him to do the Rejection Exercise, and Terry surprised himself by discovering how difficult it was for him to write the answers to some of the questions. His responses are shown in table 9.3. As with the other exercises, please pay attention to your own feelings, thoughts and actions while you read.

Table 9.3: Terry's responses to the Rejection Exercise

Where were you when you felt rejected?	At work reading an e-mail message.
What age were you?	Thirty-seven.
Who rejected you?	The company.
Why?	I made a mess of the interview.
What was said to you?	'You are not what we are looking for at this time.'
Did anyone support you?	I never told anyone.
What was it like for you to feel rejected?	Humiliating, deeply humiliating.
What happened then?	I stopped working so hard and lost interest until I left the company a year later.
What did you learn from this experience?	That it's not how hard you work that counts; instead it's who you know.

At this point in the session Terry and I moved straight on to looking at his core beliefs. He was definite that it didn't matter how hard he worked, he was never going to be good enough. My sense was that 'not good enough' was a very destructive core belief, driving Terry into self-destruction. I asked him to write on an A4 page as many examples as he could that proved he wasn't good enough.

He set to the task with gusto. He easily filled the page, referring to how terribly he had treated Nora and his three children and particularly his youngest son. He looked up at me with a sense of hopelessness. 'I'm not good enough. I've let so many people down. I've treated everyone, particularly my youngest son, so badly. I feel ashamed of myself, and I think they'd all be better off without me.'

Rather than panicking and thinking, 'Oh, no, he's talking about suicide!' I simply drew an inverted triangle on the page and filled in the thoughts, feelings and actions that Terry had mentioned. I then explained to him that thoughts such as 'people would be better off without me' and 'I'd be better off dead' can be very frightening. They can even trigger such other thoughts as 'I'm suicidal,' which can be a very frightening thought.

Terry nodded silently, surprised in acknowledgement that, yes, he had thought that he and everyone else would be better off if he was dead. I calmly asked him if he had made any plans about how he might take his own life, and his responses made it clear that he had indeed considered suicide as an option. I asked him if he knew anyone who had chosen suicide, and again he nodded: one of his closest friends had died by suicide only six months before.

Terry became distressed as he told me that he thought he was going mad. His head seemed to be invaded by thoughts telling him he was worthless and useless and that everyone would be better off if he was dead. He also had other thoughts that screamed at him to think about Nora and the children. How could they ever manage if he took his own life? He spent hours each day battling these thoughts, and he struck me as tired and worn out.

At this point in the session he completed a depression inventory and, not surprisingly, he was within the severe range of depression. He scored high on many of the items demonstrating that he was extremely self-critical and had a deep sense of worthlessness.

Terry agreed to go to his GP immediately following my session and arrange to meet a psychiatrist for assessment and treatment if this was recommended. We finished the session by looking at three Coping Sentences that would be effective in helping him deal with his depression.

— I feel hopeless because I think I've let everyone I love down, *but I choose to act in a helpful way.*
— I feel terrible because of how I think I've treated my son, *but I choose to turn things around for both of us.*
— I feel worthless because I think I'm not good enough, *but I'm more than my feelings of worthlessness.*

The Welcoming Approach is not a magic wand. It doesn't automatically make someone feel better, nor should it. Terry actually did leave my office feeling a little lighter. It was a huge relief for him to be able to tell me that he had thoughts that he would be better off dead and that he genuinely thought that he was suicidal. Now he realised that just because he had those thoughts it didn't mean that he actually was suicidal. He was relieved that he had agreed to go to his GP and to follow up with a psychiatric assessment if that was appropriate. He assured me that he would not actually harm himself but that if he thought he was at risk he would go straight to his GP or to the A&E Department of his local hospital.

Terry also agreed to concentrate on 'acting in a helpful way.' To help him do this he undertook to look at the web site of Aware (www.aware.ie). This is the national charity for supporting people who have depression and their families. As well as providing direct help in the form of support groups, the support line and the support mail service, it also provides life skills courses free of charge. Offered both in groups and on line, these use cognitive behavioural principles to help people cope with depression. The web site also has an excellent archive of lectures on such topics as depression in adolescents, depression in the elderly, and supporting the families of people who have depression.

Terry accepted my suggestion that he welcome how awful he was feeling as an indicator that he needed to act to improve things. I suggested also that this experience could prove to be a blessing in disguise. Perhaps he would be able to use his own experience of such acute distress and sense of inadequacy and hopelessness in the training of young professionals in empathy and coping skills. Maybe he would recognise signs of distress in any grandchildren he might have and be able to support them in a different way from anybody else. In suggesting this I was deliberately encouraging him to think of a time in the future when he would be alive and using his skills to contribute to the lives of people he loved. He knew he could continue to work with me to build on his coping skills and to gently look at issues from his past that may have caused him such distress.

Terry left my office with a palpable sense of hope that was very welcome to both of us!

Chapter 10

Loss

*Nothing is ever really lost to us as long as
we remember it.*

—L. M. MONTGOMERY

What happens to you when you lose something? Just imagine right now that you're packing for a trip abroad that you're going to take tomorrow. You have plenty of time and are feeling relaxed. Your clothes are washed and ready, so putting them into your luggage is satisfying. As you work, your mind is busy with your mental checklist of things to do.

But something is niggling at you. You've forgotten something. You look at what you've packed and go back through the list in your head. Everything is there, but you've definitely forgotten something. Ah, the image of your passport pops into your head and you breathe a sigh of relief. Your passport—you'd forgotten your passport. Phew! Well, that's easy to get. You always keep it safely in a particular drawer.

You can probably guess what's coming next. Yes, you go to the drawer, open it and automatically put your hand in to pull out the passport. It's not there. What happens to you next? What do you think, how do you feel and what do you do? If you're like me you'll end up sooner or later emptying everything out of the drawer to prove to yourself that it's definitely not there. You may even return to the drawer a number of times just to make sure.

At this point, a range of thoughts may be going through your head. Fig. 10.1 shows some of mine in this situation.

Fig. 10.1: Claire's Coping Triangle on not being able to find her passport

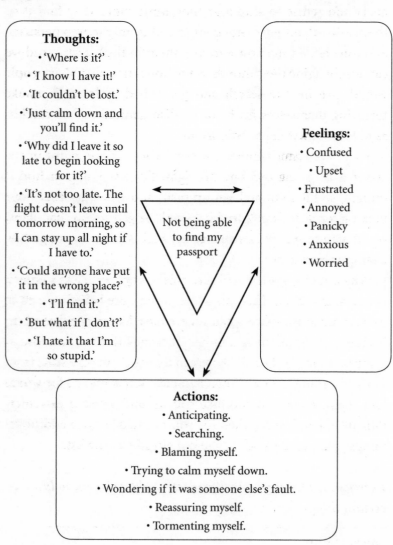

Now imagine that it's 3 a.m. You still can't find your passport, and your flight leaves at 8 a.m. What are you thinking? How do you feel? What do you do?

It can be difficult to accept that, for whatever reason, the passport is lost. Many people would continue pulling the house apart and refuse to stop searching until either they find it or they realise that they're not going to. They might even persuade everyone else in the house to join them in the search—and we can just imagine their moods as the hours tick by! Other people would give up the search and go to bed, only to lie awake torturing themselves for being so disorganised and so careless as to lose something so important.

There are some people, however, who at some point in the search will shrug and say, 'All right, I'm not going to find it tonight, so I'll go to bed, get up early, and spend another hour looking for it. If I don't find it I won't be getting on that plane, so I'll have to see if I can change my flights and sort out getting a temporary passport.'

Why is it that some people are able to cope with loss so much better than others? This can relate to our core beliefs as well as to how much we value whatever we have lost in the first place. Exercise 10.1 contains a number of things that we can lose at some point in our lives. I invite you to rate them on a scale from 1 to 5 according to how difficult you think it would be for you to lose them, 1 being not difficult at all and 5 being extremely difficult. There's space then for you to include three additional things you might lose if they're not already on the list.

Exercise 10.1: Rating how difficult it would be for me to lose certain things

An argument	
A bet	
A parking space	
A child	

A family member	
A friend	
A game	
A pet animal	
Confidence	
Jewellery	
Keys	
Money	
My eyesight	
My hair	
My health	
My home	
My job	
My life	
My memory	
My passport	
My patience	
My reputation	
My teeth	
My temper	
One of my limbs	
Promotion	
Respect for someone	
Self-respect	

If you did this exercise you might have noticed yourself hesitating and thinking, *It depends*. Our reaction to loss depends on many things. For instance, it can depend on how special the jewellery is, on how much money we're talking about, on how loved the dog, friend or family member is. So, no-one can ever fully understand the effect of a particular loss on someone, because the meaning of that loss to them and to us depends on so many things. Losing a passport might mean an inconvenient or expensive delay of a day or two; it might mean missing out on a holiday; it might mean missing an important event, such as a wedding or a funeral.

If others are directly affected by our loss too, we might experience changes in our relationships with them which can result in them being less available to support us. It can also result in us being less available for them. Coping with loss can be a very lonely experience and can lead to so many other 'little losses' we might not even realise until years later.

Loss can be overwhelming, and it can seem as if our heart is breaking. Elizabeth Kubler Ross identified patterns in people who were close to death, which she described in her book *On Death and Dying* (1969). She never meant them to be seen as 'stages of grief' that everyone must go through, reaching eventually the last stage of acceptance. Thinking that *I'm still in anger and I should be at the acceptance stage* is, in my view, unhelpful and unfair. We grieve however we grieve, and it's essential that we are gentle and compassionate with ourselves as we do so.

One wonderful book, *The Courage to Grieve* (1980) by Judy Tatlebaum, helped me to realise just how complex and raw grief is. It's a unique experience, and a very personal one.

Exercise 10.2 invites you to look at the list of various losses again and to see how often you have experienced each of them in the last year (0, not at all; 1, sometimes; 2, often; 3, a lot). This will give you an idea of how many losses, big and small, you're coping with right now.

Exercise 10.2: How often I have lost things in the past year

An argument	
A bet	
A parking space	
A child	
A family member	
A friend	
A game	
A pet animal	
Confidence	
Jewellery	
Keys	
Money	
My eyesight	
My hair	
My health	
My home	
My job	
My life	
My memory	
My passport	
My patience	
My reputation	

My teeth	
My temper	
One of my limbs	
Promotion	
Respect for someone	
Self-respect	

Sometimes it might seem easier to cope with bigger losses. We can recognise how difficult they are and show ourselves some compassion in our efforts to cope. Other people can show us understanding and give us practical support.

Coping with a range of tiny, infuriating losses can create a lot of stress that we might not even recognise. We can often be extremely hard on ourselves for how we react to a 'small' loss, and other people may not even be aware that we've lost something that's causing us distress. That may be because we're ashamed to tell them, or because we dismiss the effect the loss has had on us in the first place.

While people can be wonderfully supportive when we're coping with major loss, such as the death of someone we love, or the loss of a business or a home, they can be less tolerant when the loss is of something they consider insignificant. While they might listen sympathetically at first, they can quickly move on to reassurance, problem-solving and even brutally telling us that it's time to get over it and replace whatever it was we lost. This 'tough love' approach is usually well intentioned but can seem harsh, particularly if we've already been thinking similar thoughts ourselves.

How can we use the Welcoming Approach to help someone cope with loss? The first step of the Coping Triangle is to catch what we're thinking, how we're feeling and what we're doing in relation to whatever it is that's causing us distress. Let's do this first with two losses that we might consider minor before dealing with the greater loss of the death of someone we love.

Let's imagine that you're sitting in the waiting-room of the A&E Department of a hospital. You have a suspected broken ankle and have already been waiting more than three hours to be seen by a doctor. You think you're next in the queue when the door bursts open and a young man is rushed past you on a stretcher. Behind him runs a young woman with a baby in her arms. You realise that, regardless of how the man is and of what's wrong with him, he's going to take priority over you. You have once again lost your place. What would you think, how would you feel, and what would you do?

Depending on your level of pain and discomfort, you might think, *Oh, no, I'm going to be here for hours!* You might feel frustrated or even angry. You might sigh loudly or even complain. Probably, though, you would sit there, tell yourself that you're lucky to be as well as you are and wonder how the young man is getting on. You would instinctively cope with the loss of your place by considering it less important than the possible loss of life or limb for that young man.

Compare this situation with you waiting patiently until a car leaves its parking space. It's a busy Saturday afternoon, you've spent twenty minutes driving round the car park looking for a space, and finally you've spotted an elderly couple loading up their car. They seem to take for ever as they wave goodbye to friends, put in their various bags, settle in, put on their seat-belts, wave at someone else, open the window for a chat; then finally they're off. As you turn on your ignition to drive into the space they've just left you realise that someone else has beaten you to it. Somehow, as you looked down to turn your key, someone else had brazenly driven into your space. Now, how would you feel, what would you think, and what would you do? You might feel a sense of shock and disbelief as you think, *I don't believe this!* You could well feel angry. What would you do, though?

Coping with loss seems easier somehow when the loss is recognised as being big and we get support. We often underestimate just how significant 'tiny' losses can be. If they're not dealt with they can rob us of a healthy sense of self-respect as well as an opportunity to practise coping. We could take so many examples: the horror of the loss of life in the Twin Towers in New York compared with the upset of a twelve-year-old when his school team loses the final because he let in the winning goal; the distress of losing a treasured piece of jewellery compared with the finality of losing a friend through suicide. We might think our 'tiny' losses can't be compared to the bigger ones, and so we often learn to cope by minimising them and saying that 'they were only small things anyway.'

How many sports people have been told to pick themselves up after losing, as 'there's always another opportunity in the future'? How many women have been told to cope with the loss of a baby by 'counting their blessings,' that they're young, or that they have other children? People don't say things like that to be deliberately cruel: instead they're usually doing the best they can to make the person 'feel better.'

As we know only too well, the comments and opinions of other people can hurt, particularly if we're feeling vulnerable already. Whether this hurt is because they deliberately intended to upset us or because we misinterpret what they said and took it personally, we need to be respectful of our own feelings of hurt and loss.

Let's see how the Coping Triangle provides a respectful, powerful framework for helping people to acknowledge their feelings about their loss, become aware of their thoughts as being 'helpful' or 'unhelpful', unearth and question their core beliefs and then, very deliberately, concentrate on helpful actions they can do.

Exercise 10.3 provides you with the opportunity to write what you think your thoughts, feelings and actions might be if you lost your space in a hospital waiting-room and your parking space in a car park. For ease of comparison I have presented step 1 of the Coping Triangle in a table rather than in two triangles.

Often we take ourselves by surprise in our own responses to loss. An interesting experiment is to ask someone who knows you well to complete exercise 10.3 according to how they think you would think, feel and act in these two situations. You might be surprised, and it could lead to a very interesting conversation!

Exercise 10.3: How I think I would think, feel and act in response to two different losses

	Thoughts	Feelings	Actions
Losing a space in the hospital waiting-room			
Losing a parking space in the car park			

I asked a few people how they thought they might feel, what they might think and what they might do in both these situations. Interestingly, how they told me they would feel and how they would think were very similar; there were big differences, though, in the actions they told me they would take. Of course just because we say, 'This is what I would do,' doesn't mean that we would actually do that! Hopefully, the people who said they would react in an aggressive way would show more self-control if the occasion did arise.

The feelings, thoughts and range of actions of the people I asked are listed in table 10.1. As you read, see how many of these match your own. (You may also wonder if there were differences in the age or gender of the people who responded to my questions. There were, but as this was not a scientific research study I'm not going to say what they were!)

Table 10.1: How some people thought they would think, feel and act in response to two different losses

	Thoughts	Feelings	Actions
Losing a space in the hospital waiting-room	• 'Ah, no!' • 'I don't believe this!' • 'It's not fair.' • 'I've been here hours already.' • 'Does anyone actually care about me?'	• Annoyed • Frustrated • Fed up • Self-pity • Self-disgust	• Moan and groan. • Attack oneself brutally for feeling annoyed, frustrated, fed up and self-pitying.

	Thoughts	Feelings	Actions
Losing a space in the hospital waiting-room, *contd*.	• 'Just shut up complaining. He seems to be badly hurt. He may even be dead or dying. That's just like you. Typical, wanting attention and not even thinking about someone else. You're pathetic!'		• Assure the staff that you're happy to wait all night to be seen, and that if there's anything you can do to support the family of the young man who was brought in you're happy to do that. • Leave and go home, intending to return later.
Losing a parking space in the car park	• 'What? I don't believe this.' • 'They can't be serious!' • 'There's no way they're getting away with this.' • 'Are they blind?'	• Furious • Shocked	• Beep the horn loudly. • Curse. • Open the window and shout or scream abuse.

	Thoughts	Feelings	Actions
	• 'Who do they think they are?'		• Park in front and refuse to leave when they want [i.e. act like a child who hasn't got his or her own way!]. • Leave the car park and go somewhere else. • Cry.

Are you a little shocked at the suggestion of blocking the other car? It does seem extreme; but while we can often cope graciously when faced with major stresses, we can surprise ourselves with how childish we can become in coping with the little ones. Also, while the action may be childish, someone could easily be hurt as a result of this confrontation. So this is a great example to use to see how the person could have coped differently!

All right, that's step 1 of the Coping Triangle. As we've seen, catching what we think, how we feel and what we do can make us feel better but may not necessarily do so. Step 2, then, requires us to ask our four questions:

1. Do the feelings make sense?
2. Are the thoughts helpful or unhelpful?
3. What does he or she believe?
4. Are the actions helpful or unhelpful?

While we may not agree that the feelings of the people I asked are 'appropriate', I see them as making complete sense. First of all, both situations involved a long wait, followed by a sharp and unexpected disappointment, so we might expect the people involved to feel aggrieved. When we then consider the thoughts, we can see each feeling as making absolute sense. If any of us have thoughts about how unfairly we've been treated we'll feel upset or frustrated.

I would consider each of the thoughts to be unhelpful, and perhaps you may agree with me. While some of these thoughts may be understandable, they are unhelpful, as they cause the person to feel worse.

The third question is interesting, though. What do you think he or she believes? (I've deliberately not specified whether the person is a man or a woman, as that might influence us in our own interpretation of these two situations.) For instance, does it seem more frightening, or more childish, for a man to react violently in the car park than for a woman? People who react aggressively to being kept waiting may believe they have to fight to get what they want. This contrasts with people who willingly allow everyone else in the waiting-room to go ahead of them because they believe they don't count and that other people have greater needs.

Regardless of what the person believes, the essential thing is how they react and whether those actions are 'helpful' or 'unhelpful'. The action that I consider particularly unhelpful in the hospital waiting-room is the savage personal self-attack, with thoughts such as 'Shut up complaining', 'Typical' and 'You're pathetic'. There is absolutely no self-compassion or understanding shown. Perhaps the person who is verbally abusive in the car park might also attack himself or herself later when the shock of his or her behaviour kicks in. It's easy to see how acting like an angry child is unhelpful, though possibly there are moments when each of us is tempted to do the same.

It's not enough to do only the first two steps of the Coping Triangle, i.e. catching what we think, how we feel and what we do and asking ourselves the four questions: it's essential that we complete the third step and create a strong and powerful Coping Sentence. Here are two that I think may be of help:

— I feel frustrated / fed up / angry because I've been waiting so long, and now it looks as if I'll have to wait even longer, *but I'm grateful that I have only something relatively minor wrong with me.*

— I feel absolutely furious, because I think that person has a cheek to take my car space, *but I choose to breathe slowly and consider my options before I react.*

The Coping Sentence provides a structure in which to really acknowledge feelings instead of denying them, burying them or lashing out inappropriately because of them. It acknowledges them as making sense by linking them with the predominant thoughts. Its power then is in shifting focus to consider how to act proactively.

If the person in the hospital waiting-room concentrated on 'counting their blessings' and being grateful for having only something minor wrong with them, without acknowledging the feelings of frustration and annoyance, those feelings would get buried, only to resurface at what might be an inappropriate time in the future.

Breathing slowly really does work in providing a moment of sanity in particularly stressful situations, such as the incident in the car park. A powerful and simple exercise is to breathe in while tightening the muscles in your non-dominant hand. If you like you could try it right now as you're reading this. Breathe in while tightening the muscles in your hand; hold your breath and your hand tightly for three seconds, then release them both. Do this twice more.

Now do the exercise again, but this time as you're breathing in deliberately think this thought: *I choose to breathe slowly.* Hold your breath for three seconds, then breathe out.

Did you notice that without any obvious effort on your part you actually did breathe more slowly during the second round of three than the first? This demonstrates the power of the word 'choose'. If I had suggested that you think *I have to breathe slowly* you may have felt some pressure rather than automatically breathing more slowly.

How we cope with small and relatively minor losses will influence how we cope with larger ones. Loss is very much a part of life; and probably the greatest loss that any of us can experience is the death of someone we love. It used to be thought that children and adults who have learning disabilities did not notice when someone they loved died. It makes so much sense to know that this is not so.

How we react to the loss of someone we love can depend on many things, called variables. Table 10.2 lists some of these and has space in which you can include other variables that you see as important that may not be already there.

Table 10.2: Some variables that can affect how we cope with the death of someone we love

---

- Our age
- Our relationship with the person who has died
- Our previous experiences of loss and death
- The support we have available to us
- Our ability to take the support that's available to us
- The age of the person who has died

- How the person died
- The attitude that the person we loved had towards death
- Our financial circumstances before and after the death
- Whether we have spiritual or religious beliefs

I would like to give you two examples from my own life to illustrate how using the Welcoming Approach helped me cope with the loss of two people I loved very much. The first was in March 2001. My mother and I were standing outside the intensive care unit of a Dublin hospital being told by a doctor that my Aunty Noreen was gravely ill and might not survive the night. Noreen was eleven years older than my mother; she was like a second mother to her, and she was much more than an aunt to me. While I could give many examples of her love and support for me, perhaps the one that sums it all up is the time she told me that she would always be 'in my corner.' It didn't matter what I did: she wanted me to know that I could always count on her to be on my side, in my corner. This still stands out as one of the greatest and most precious gifts I have ever been given.

Hearing the doctor tell us that Noreen might die within the next few hours was shocking and deeply upsetting. I remember the many thoughts rushing into my head competing to be heard, thoughts such as *No, that's not fair; I don't want Aunty Noreen to die; What will I do without her?* Within seconds my attention was directed to how awful my life would be without her. I could picture her funeral, and in those moments I felt a terrible loneliness and a deep sense of loss.

I made a decision as I stood listening to the doctor that I was not going to waste one moment of the time that Aunty Noreen was alive worrying about how I was going to be when she died. From then until her death three weeks later, any time I had thoughts of how awful life would be for me when she died I firmly told myself, 'But I still have her now.' Without realising it, I was doing my very best to live mindfully in the present moment. It wasn't easy, but I found those few words to be hugely powerful in helping me to switch from thinking about my imminent loss to appreciating and supporting my aunt.

The biggest surprise of my life was that my experience of my Aunty Noreen's actual death was magical, certainly not what I had expected at all. It was an enormous privilege for me to share her final moments with her and with the other members of my family who also deeply loved her. Then the feelings of sadness, loss, upset, fear, loneliness and anger all flowed in. Over the next few weeks I often needed to stop my car to allow my tears to flow and to allow myself to howl in grief. I was greatly relieved that I had read Judy Tatlebaum's book *The Courage to Grieve* years before, so that I knew that I was not going mad. I knew that my grief was so raw because I loved Noreen so much, and somewhere inside me I knew that the raw pain would become less intense eventually and that I needed to be gentle with myself during this time. The Coping Sentence that I used over and over and that worked each time for me was:

I feel lonely / sad / terrible / awful because Aunty Noreen has died, and I miss her so much, *but I was blessed to have had her in my life.*

The truth of those few words helped me every single time to focus on my gratitude and stopped the barrage of cruel thoughts of loss. This Coping Sentence may not work at all for you, so it's important to take time to devise one that's effective for you.

The second example of how I used the Welcoming Approach to help me cope with loss is my father's death, seven years after

Noreen's. I knew that my feelings of distress, loss, upset, sadness and loneliness made sense because of the close relationship I was blessed to have with him. I knew, even as I was thinking them, that a lot of the thoughts I had were unhelpful. I knew too that no matter what I thought he was not going to come back. My own spiritual and religious beliefs proved a huge source of support to me, as I really believed that my father's spirit had not gone too far away and that somehow he was close. None of us actually know whether this is so, but I found it more comforting to believe it than not. The thing that helped me most was the relationship that I had had with my father and the knowledge that he was at peace with his own death. He had struggled with cancer for so long, and I didn't want to see him suffer any more.

One of the hardest things about my father's death was witnessing the intense sadness of everyone who had loved him as they came to terms with their loss. I did my best to act in a way that was helpful, but the thing that helped me most was finding and then using two powerful Coping Sentences. I still use them when intense feelings of loss rise up unexpectedly. The first is the same one I used when my Aunty Noreen died. It was so true and it did help:

I feel lonely / sad / terrible / awful because Dad has died, and I miss him so much, *but I was blessed to have had him in my life.*

It was often not powerful enough, though, as other thoughts tended to come in, such as *Yes, but I still miss him,* which brought me back to my feeling of loss. The following one worked much better for me:

I feel lonely / sad / terrible / awful because Dad has died, and I miss him so much, *but his suffering is over.*

I encourage you to spend as long as it takes for you to come up with your own Coping Sentences. The most powerful words to come after the 'but' will be the ones that are true and that give you an immediate sense of relief. These words are very individual, and I encourage you to take some time to find the ones that work best for you.

I'm very aware that as you read this I have no idea what losses you are coping with right now. I don't think anyone can say that any one loss is easier to cope with than any other. As we have seen, it depends on many things.

Probably one of the hardest losses that anyone has to face is the death of a child. It seems so wrong, as instinctively we can all think that a child is born to live to old age. We know this is not always true, though. Some who are conceived do not survive in the womb, as a result of a miscarriage or an abortion; those who survive may be born healthy or ill; those who are ill may die soon after birth, and their loss can have just as severe an impact on their parents as the death of an older child who dies tragically.

If we are in the position of supporting someone who is struggling to cope with the death of a child, it's important to remember that feelings of sadness make sense.

It's all right for any of us to feel sad when we're witnessing the deep distress of someone we love, particularly when we know that nothing we can say or do can take their feelings of distress away. Sometimes it's simply all right just to feel sad.

What if we lose someone as a result of suicide? Very few people can know or understand why someone chose to end their life. We do know that many people who choose suicide had alcohol in their system, which may have affected their actions. The pain of grief can be much harder when the people who are left to cope torture themselves with question after question. *Why did they choose suicide? Why did they not talk to someone who could have helped? How did I not know? Why didn't I ... ?*

The word 'welcome' might jar with people who have been bereaved through suicide. I'm not at all suggesting that anyone could or should welcome the death of someone through suicide. The Welcoming Approach can be of help, however, in assisting us to realise that feelings of deep and intense loss and distress make sense; that such thoughts as *why?* are often unhelpful; that beliefs such as *I didn't do enough* may not be true (they're usually not); and that actions can be helpful or unhelpful. It can be very difficult to get a Coping Sentence that will give an immediate sense of relief. However, often we genuinely don't know how strong we are until we need to be. One of the most helpful Coping Sentences can be:

> I feel torn apart because I don't know why they chose suicide, and I think that maybe I could have done something to have prevented it, *but somehow I will get through this.*

Reminding ourselves that somehow we'll get through even the most difficult of times can be the one tiny bit of support that actually does help and can distract us from the many unhelpful thoughts we might have.

The loss of a passport fades into insignificance when compared with the death of someone we love. But how we cope with the 'little' losses helps us to cope with the more challenging ones. Rather than tormenting ourselves each time we lose something small, let's practise being gentle and understanding, saying something like:

> I feel frustrated because I've lost something and can't find it, *but I choose to treat myself with gentleness and compassion.*

Chapter 11
Failure and success

Failure is success in progress.

—ALBERT EINSTEIN

The nature of life is that we will cope with some of its challenges much better than with others. Some we will take in our stride and masterfully glide our way through. We will know that there's real support there and we will willingly and gratefully take that support.

One of life's certainties is that there will be other times when we will struggle. We will wonder why we're in the difficult situation in the first place. We may isolate ourselves from others, pretend that everything is fine and absolutely refuse even a hint of help from anyone else. We will probably blame ourselves harshly and we may even consider that life is too much and we may consider giving up.

A habit that's easy enough to get into is comparing what we have and what we do with other people around us. It's a habit that can get out of control and can lead to dissatisfaction and unease.

Albert Einstein is a great role model for all of us. He didn't seem to believe in failure. He is reported to have said when he was asked about failing yet again in inventing the light bulb that he hadn't failed but had instead discovered another way that didn't work. There's a difference between the challenge of coping with what we perceive as failure and the fear that we might fail. It may seem bizarre that success could possibly be one of life's challenges but, tragically, too many people have stumbled and fallen as a result of an inability to cope with success.

Why? Why can it be so hard for us to cope with 'failure' and 'success'?

Let's take 'failure' first. I'm deliberately putting it in quotation marks, as people's perceptions of failure may not match reality. I've been privileged to work with people who I see as extremely successful in many ways. Many of them arrived to my office burdened down by what they described as 'failure'.

I present here the story of a young woman, whom I have called Chloe, to represent how the Welcoming Approach can be used in practice. (As with the other people I refer to in this book, Chloe is not a real person. However, her concerns are similar in many ways to those of people I have had the privilege to work with.)

CHLOE

Chloe was twenty-three when she was referred to me by her GP to help her with her anxiety about university. She arrived for our first meeting apologising profusely that she was ten minutes late. She began to cry and told me that she was so sorry for being late, that it was completely her fault, as she had taken the wrong road. She muttered quietly to herself, 'Typical! When did I ever do anything right?' It was clear that she was under considerable pressure, and I suspected that most of it was self-generated.

Chloe described what had brought her to her GP and then in turn to me. She was the youngest of three children, born six years after her twin sisters, who worked in good jobs, were in secure relationships and had 'everything going for them.' Chloe's mother was a nurse and her father was the principal of a secondary school. She described them both as having been very patient and supportive. Her years in primary school were fine. She was a 'high achiever' who always did well. She made good friends and is still in contact with three of them.

Chloe's move to secondary school was difficult, as she was identified within minutes as being the principal's daughter. Her sisters had taken all that natural teasing in their stride, Chloe told me, but somehow she wasn't able for it. Her friends were in a different class and seemed to settle in quickly. Chloe found her first three years in secondary school to be very difficult. She became quiet and shy and wasn't confident around her peers. She assumed that the other pupils didn't trust her and thought she went home in the evenings and discussed them with her father. She wasn't really sure when she had first thought that but could remember doing her best to explain to her classmates that she never talked about them when she was at home. She shrugged, embarrassed, as she described their cold, sarcastic reactions.

Without realising it, Chloe began to feel deeply unhappy most of the time. She was still able to perform well in school, and no-one really seemed to notice that she was becoming quieter and quieter. She didn't realise that she had developed poor study habits, and instead of getting through her school work quickly she tended to daydream. She described her first state exam, her Junior Cert, as 'grand at the time' and was shocked when, instead of coming at the top of her class, as she had always done, she found she hadn't done well in three of her subjects. She blushed with embarrassment as she described the hurtful comment of one of her classmates who said, 'Oh, Daddy won't be pleased with your results, will he!'

Chloe was so distressed that she unconsciously began to scratch her left arm as a means of comfort. She found that if she hurt herself enough she experienced some relief. Her actions distracted her from her feelings of anxiety, and she became an expert at finding tools to hurt herself with while at the same time successfully hiding her scars. She didn't realise the dangerous path of addictive self-harm she had started down; all she knew was that she had discovered a way of making herself feel better.

She didn't know that some of her classmates had found other dangerous ways of distracting themselves from their feelings until one of them died as a result of bulimia. Her years of secret binge-eating and purging had completely upset her system and caused her to die from a heart attack when she was only sixteen years old.

Chloe cried as she told me how frightened she had been while attending her classmate's funeral. She knew that cutting herself as a way of coping with pressure was wrong and went to her school guidance counsellor for help. She told me that she was terrified of her parents' reactions and begged the guidance counsellor not to tell her father. Thankfully, the guidance counsellor knew that he needed to be told and did so in what sounded like a very sensitive way.

Her parents and sisters were shocked, as they had no idea that Chloe felt so unhappy. Her sisters felt guilty for not having noticed the extent of the pressure she had been under and wanted to 'rescue' her by encouraging their parents to move her to another school. Chloe told me that she disagreed with this plan. She only had two more years of secondary school to get through and she thought that moving school wouldn't make her feel any more confident. She was referred by her GP to the Child and Adolescent Mental Health Services, where she received help and learnt to respond to feelings of upset and distress in a way that was healthy and safe for her.

As Chloe described important events in her life I was struck by how easily she dismissed any successes and concentrated instead on telling me in detail of the many 'failures' she had had. For instance, she did exceptionally well in her Leaving Cert but only, according to Chloe, because she had brilliant teachers. She saw her success as having nothing to do with how hard she worked.

Her excellent results meant that she was eligible to study practically anything in university, but her lack of confidence meant that she applied for courses that she knew had minimum entrance requirements. Within six weeks she knew she had made the wrong choice. She had absolutely no interest in what she was supposed to be studying, but she decided she could stick with it for four years and then do a postgraduate course and qualify as a secondary teacher. That thought filled her with horror, as she imagined herself back working in her own school, being compared by pupils, parents and teachers with her father. With sudden clarity she knew she wasn't going to do that.

Chloe became embarrassed as she described 'dropping out' of university. She went to France to work as an au pair, which she loved. Then a year later she returned to university to study languages with a view to being a professional interpreter. I noticed that once again she seemed to minimise how well she had coped with a situation that could have been very difficult. She looked uncomfortable when I mentioned this and quickly told me that she was very lucky when she was in France. She worked with a lovely family who were very good to her.

Can you see her patterns of blaming herself for everything that had gone wrong in her life and either dismissing any possible success, minimising it or attributing it to someone else? So why was Chloe in my office with an invisible but very present sign hanging round her neck saying *I'm a complete and total failure.*

She finished with a first-class honours degree, and the following year, with her lecturers' encouragement, she began studying for a PhD. 'My PhD work is going fine. I'll be finished it next year, and I already have a job offer in Brussels that seems exciting.'

She looked at me with fresh tears gathering and said, 'You're probably wondering why I've ended up here. I'm so stupid. I was well warned, and I didn't listen. I fell in love, gave my heart away, got dumped and somehow just can't pick myself up again.' She sobbed as she told me how stunned she had been when another student had asked her out. She had had a few 'disaster' dates when she was a teenager and had decided that she was just not 'good girl-friend material.' She really liked this man, Mark, and was thrilled when they seemed to click. Her sisters didn't like him, saying he was 'a bit too slick', but Chloe thought they were just jealous, as he really was 'perfect'.

We don't need to go into lots of detail: suffice it to say that Mark said he was bored with Chloe and wanted to experiment sexually. She described feeling shocked when he introduced her to 'a friend' and said that he wanted the three of them to experience together what he had experienced with both of them separately. The other woman obviously knew about his suggestion and was willing to go along with it. Chloe didn't know what shocked her more, the fact that Mark obviously had some sort of a sexual relationship with another woman that she knew nothing about or that he wanted to involve her in a threesome. She described just walking away without saying one word to either of them.

Now, three months later, she has been torturing herself for not having dealt with things better. She didn't really know what she would have done differently, but she was clear that 'every other woman would have known what to do, instead of stupidly walking away as if it didn't matter.' She had lost interest in her research and was close to tears most of the time. She had deliberately avoided family gatherings, as she thought the pressure to be 'normal' would be too much. While her excuse of being 'too busy' had worked so far, she knew it was only a matter of time before one or other of her sisters arrived, demanding to know what was wrong with her and why she was upsetting her parents so much.

Chloe blushed as she said, 'I suppose as I'm here I should tell you everything,' and she silently rolled up her left sleeve. The fresh wounds had not yet begun to heal and it was obvious that she had very recently cut herself. 'I hate that I'm doing this again,' Chloe whispered, 'after all that help I got too. I was so proud of myself when I was doing my degree that no matter how much pressure I was under I never cut myself. And now, here I am falling to pieces and cutting myself to pieces over a stupid break-up. I would have thought I had more sense.'

When I asked her if there was anything else she wanted me to know before we moved to look at how the Welcoming Approach might help her, Chloe nodded and said, 'I'm so afraid that I won't be able to stop cutting myself. When I do it I get such satisfaction; it feels so good, and I don't really want to stop it.'

Sometimes when people trust me with their story and share such personal details with me they feel some relief and may already feel a bit better. Many times, though, people like Chloe can become overwhelmed by how 'ridiculous' they are to be 'making such a big deal' of whatever is going on. They may experience an acute sense of shame, and they may judge themselves even more harshly. When I told Chloe that I wouldn't be surprised if she actually felt worse after telling me everything, she nodded her agreement.

She was willing to use the three steps of the Coping Triangle and explained that, even though she didn't think anything could help her feel better about herself, she was willing to give it a go.

The first step was for Chloe to choose something that was bothering her and then catch her thoughts, feelings and actions in relation to this and write them down. As she was clearly so upset I suggested that we look at what was going on for her right then, just after she had told me her story. At this point she sat with her head down looking lost. It seemed clear to me that she didn't really want to feel better. She had judged herself as being useless, stupid and a failure, and her punishment was self-torture for some time to come. What was her crime? In her eyes it was 'being so stupid'!

Before we examine Chloe's thoughts, feelings and actions, take a few moments to see how you are right now. Are you relating to Chloe, feeling compassion and understanding towards her? Are you feeling puzzled, wondering why she's not celebrating being well away from someone who didn't treat her properly? If you're thinking you have no interest in Chloe or her story you may be feeling bored or frustrated. Please take a moment to catch your own thoughts, feelings and actions in the first step of the Coping Triangle, which is in fig. 11.1. Chloe's thoughts, feelings and actions are shown in fig. 11.2.

Fig. 11.1: Step 1 of my coping triangle on reading Chloe's story

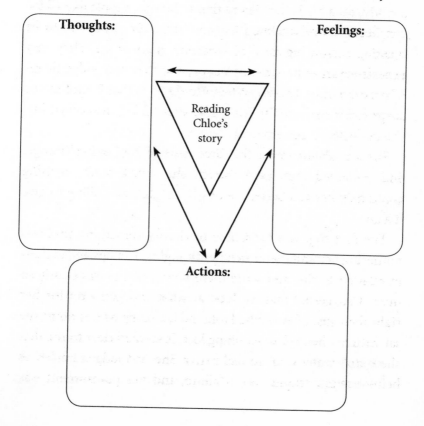

Thoughts:

Feelings:

Reading
Chloe's
story

Actions:

Fig. 11.2: Step 1 of Chloe's Coping Triangle

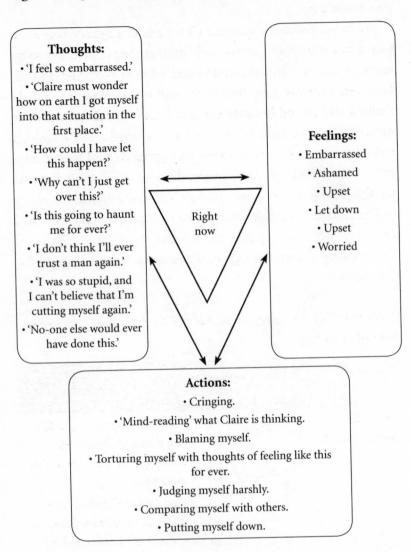

Thoughts:
- 'I feel so embarrassed.'
- 'Claire must wonder how on earth I got myself into that situation in the first place.'
- 'How could I have let this happen?'
- 'Why can't I just get over this?'
- 'Is this going to haunt me for ever?'
- 'I don't think I'll ever trust a man again.'
- 'I was so stupid, and I can't believe that I'm cutting myself again.'
- 'No-one else would ever have done this.'

Feelings:
- Embarrassed
- Ashamed
- Upset
- Let down
- Upset
- Worried

Right now

Actions:
- Cringing.
- 'Mind-reading' what Claire is thinking.
- Blaming myself.
- Torturing myself with thoughts of feeling like this for ever.
- Judging myself harshly.
- Comparing myself with others.
- Putting myself down.

As Chloe and I discussed her actions I told her that she seemed to me to be doing something else also. She had recognised that she wasn't feeling good, and she had taken active steps to feel better by making an appointment to see me. 'The only snag is,' I told her, 'that you don't really think anything can help you.' Chloe nodded and with a slight smile told me that I was reading her mind.

When we looked at whether Chloe's feelings made sense she was very clear that they did not. She said she was too old to be reacting like a 'broken-hearted sixteen-year-old.' She agreed, however, with my view that if she had been feeling absolutely thrilled and proud because she had begun to cut herself once more I would be worried. My point was simple: while Chloe's feelings were raw, very painful, very difficult and distressing, every one of them actually made sense according to what was going on for her or because of what she was thinking.

The next step in the process was to look at each of Chloe's thoughts, one by one, and see whether they were helpful or unhelpful. She decided that each of them was unhelpful, for the reasons given in table 11.1.

Table 11.1: Chloe's responses about whether her thoughts were helpful or unhelpful

Thoughts	Helpful or unhelpful?	Reasons
'I feel so embarrassed.'	U	1. Chloe already knew she felt embarrassed. Repeatedly thinking it caused her to feel even worse. 2. There was an assumption that there was something wrong with her for feeling embarrassed.

Thoughts	Helpful or unhelpful?	Reasons
'Claire must wonder how on earth I got myself into that situation in the first place.'	U	1. This thought caused Chloe to feel embarrassed. 2. She was judging herself very harshly. 3. She was assuming that Claire was thinking the worst.
'How could I have let this happen?'	U	1. This wasn't really a question but more 'I shouldn't have let this happen,' which was a judgement and didn't make her feel good. 2. When Chloe thought this she felt upset. 3. This thought reinforced the idea that what had happened was Chloe's fault.
'Why can't I just get over this?'	U	1. The more Chloe asked herself this question, the worse she felt. 2. She was assuming that what happened to her was something that she should just get over, and that because she couldn't there was something wrong with her.

Thoughts	Helpful or unhelpful?	Reasons
'Is this going to haunt me for ever?'	U	1. This thought caused Chloe to feel frightened and distressed. 2. When she thought this the automatic answer was 'yes.' She then thought of a future in which she was haunted by her difficult experience, which, not surprisingly, resulted in her feeling worse.
'I don't think I'll ever trust a man again.'	U	1. This thought caused Chloe to feel upset and distressed. 2. It catapulted her into a future full of distrust of men, which didn't make her feel good.
'I was so stupid, and I can't believe that I'm cutting myself again.'	U	1. The first part of this thought is very judgemental and didn't make her feel good. 2. The second part was not in fact true. Chloe knew she was cutting again, but the thought was unhelpful, because it didn't make her feel good about herself.

Thoughts	Helpful or unhelpful?	Reasons
'No-one else would have done this.'	U	1. This thought didn't make her feel good. 2. Chloe didn't actually know whether or not this was true. She was making an assumption that reinforces her belief that she is stupid.

As we discussed each of Chloe's thoughts in turn she became exasperated, saying, 'They're all unhelpful. No wonder I'm in such a mess! What happened was bad enough, but here I am making things even worse. I'm so, so stupid!' I asked her how she was feeling as she said this and she stopped for a moment and said slowly, 'I feel even worse, so I suppose that what I was just thinking and said aloud was unhelpful too.' When I asked her why, she said, 'Because I felt even worse.'

At this point in the process Chloe was clearly intrigued. Sounding a bit surprised, she told me that it seemed logical. She looked at me and, with a hint of hope in her voice, asked me what the third question was. I asked her to choose her most frequent thought. She smiled and said, 'I suppose it has to be that I'm stupid.' When I asked her what was so bad about being stupid she looked puzzled and said, 'Because I just am.' She clearly believed that she was stupid. However, fig. 11.3 illustrates how using the Downward Arrow technique helped her to discover something else that she deeply believed was true about herself.

Fig. 11.3: Chloe's process in discovering her core beliefs

	I'm so stupid.
What's so bad about that?	↓
	Because I just am.
What's so bad about that?	↓
	I shouldn't be so stupid.
What's so bad about that?	↓
	I'm letting everyone down.
What's so bad about that?	↓
	I'm not good enough.

At this point Chloe began to cry. She told me that she really did believe she wasn't good enough and would never be good enough. As she spoke, it became clear to both of us that she also believed that because she was stupid and not good enough she was a failure. With a forced laugh, she said, 'The ultimate proof that I'm a failure is that I got myself into a relationship with Mark in the first place. I didn't see the warning signs that my sisters spotted. I ignored them and did my own thing anyway, and look where that got me!'

We could have spent quite a while exploring when or how she began to believe this, which might or might not have been helpful. We didn't do this, though. Knowing that Chloe was going to resist any attempt by me to convince her that she was intelligent and had succeeded in many areas of her life, I simply said, 'Maybe you are good enough.' I explained that while she believed, deeply believed, that she was a failure, maybe she was in fact a success, just as some people believed the world was flat and it actually isn't.

Several things from Chloe's story had struck me as proof of how resilient, strong, intelligent and courageous she was. She didn't need to agree with me, but maybe what I was saying was true.

Let's go over her story again, concentrating on what might contradict her belief of not being good enough, as listed in table 11.2.

Table 11.2: Points from Chloe's story that contradict her belief that she is a failure

---

- She acted on her GP's recommendation to get some help and support.
- She arrived for the meeting, even though she was upset about being late. Somebody else might have decided not to bother.
- Her years in primary school were fine.
- She made good friends, which she still has.
- She asked for help from her guidance counsellor.
- She chose to stay in her secondary school despite her sisters' recommendation that she move school.
- She took help from the Child and Adolescent Mental Health Services.
- She stopped cutting herself.
- She did exceptionally well in her Leaving Cert.
- She recognised quickly that she was doing the wrong subject in university and decided to leave.
- She was clear that she wasn't going to become a teacher and work in the school she had attended.
- She went to France for a year and loved working as an au pair.
- She returned to university to do something she was interested in, with a clear sense of purpose regarding her future career.
- Her PhD work was going well.
- She has a job offer that seems exciting.

- She went out with Mark regardless of her sisters' reservations.
- She recognised quickly that she didn't want to go along with Mark's suggestion.
- She calmly and quietly walked away.
- She chose to be completely honest and reveal that she had recently begun cutting herself again.
- She recognised how strong she was to have coped with the stresses of her studies without falling back into the pattern of cutting again.
- She recognised the danger in getting satisfaction from cutting herself.

As Chloe described her story, it was clear that she was very self-critical. Answering the fourth question required her to concentrate carefully on each of her actions and consider carefully whether they were helpful or unhelpful. First she did this on the actions she had listed during the first step of the Coping Triangle, and her responses are shown in table 11.3.

Table 11.3: Chloe's responses about whether her actions were helpful or unhelpful, with Claire's comments

Chloe's actions	Helpful or unhelpful?	Claire's comments
Cringing.	Unhelpful	Cringing reinforced Chloe's low self-esteem.
'Mind-reading' what Claire is thinking.	Unhelpful	We can all do this, but we have no way of knowing whether the way we imagine people are thinking is correct. This was unhelpful for Chloe, as she was assuming that I was thinking badly of her, which caused her to feel worse.

Chloe's actions	Helpful or unhelpful?	Claire's comments
Blaming herself.	Unhelpful	It can be automatic for people who believe they are not good enough to blame themselves for anything and everything that goes wrong. This can be unhelpful, as it just makes them feel even worse, and they can too easily slip into a self-punitive pattern. There are occasions when we do something that is actually our fault. Rather than blaming ourselves for having done this, it's usually more helpful for us to take responsibility for our actions and to concentrate on what helpful actions we can then take.
Torturing herself with thoughts of feeling like this for ever.	Unhelpful	We've seen how easy it is for thoughts to trigger feelings. It can be bad enough for any one of us to feel unhappy, sad, upset, lonely, angry or distressed; how much worse, then, is it for us to imagine that we're going to feel like this for ever? Without even realising that we're doing it, such thoughts can prompt us to feel a deep sense of helplessness and even hopelessness. Self-torture is definitely not helpful!

Chloe's actions	Helpful or unhelpful?	Claire's comments
Judging herself harshly.	Unhelpful	Professional judges are trained to impartially consider the context of an event and to consider what is 'reasonable' behaviour within certain agreed rules. Chloe's self-judgement is completely biased and cruelly harsh. It's unhelpful because it's unfair. Most of us are our own worst critics. This is unhelpful because it causes her to feel even worse. It's also unhelpful because it adds more confirmation to her belief that she is a failure.
Comparing herself with others.	Unhelpful	Comparing ourselves with others or with how we think we 'should' be is a very common action. It's not helpful, though, as it made Chloe feel worse. She was very unlikely to find anyone she could compare herself with who would make her feel better.

Chloe's actions	Helpful or unhelpful?	Claire's comments
Putting herself down.	Unhelpful	Picture two lovely three-year-old children showing you pictures they have just drawn. Now see yourself looking at them for a moment and saying, 'Is that the best you can do? You've used the wrong colours, and the whole thing is a terrible mess.' Can you imagine the reaction of those two little children? How could Chloe be surprised that she didn't feel good when she treated herself so badly?

Chloe looked at me sadly at this point and said, 'Not surprisingly, all my actions are unhelpful. No wonder I've felt so bad!' Can you see how she was continuing to look for proof that she was a failure? She was surprised when I smiled and said there were many other actions that she was doing so automatically that she didn't even realise she was doing them. Some of these were actions that I had seen her do since we met; others were actions she had described while she was telling me her story. Chloe agreed to consider whether each of these additional actions was helpful or unhelpful. We took time to consider each one carefully. Her responses, along with my comments, are shown in table 11.4.

Table 11.4: Chloe's responses to whether her additional actions were helpful or unhelpful, together with Claire's comments

Chloe's actions	Helpful or unhelpful?	Claire's comments
Apologising for being ten minutes late.	Helpful / Unhelpful	Many of us were taught as children that if we do something wrong we need to apologise. I see the act of apologising as unhelpful if we do it excessively, particularly if we haven't done anything wrong in the first place. It was probably helpful for Chloe to apologise once for being late, as it was courteous. However, apologising profusely, as she did, was unhelpful, as it reinforced her idea that she was a failure.
'Mind-reading' what Claire was thinking.	Unhelpful	We can all do this, but we have no way of knowing whether the way we imagine people are thinking is correct. This was unhelpful for Chloe, as she was assuming that I was thinking badly of her, which caused her to feel worse.
Comparing herself with her sisters.	Unhelpful	When Chloe compared herself with her sisters she felt worthless in comparison. So comparing herself with them was clearly not helpful for her!

Chloe's actions	Helpful or unhelpful?	Claire's comments
Working hard in primary school.	Helpful	Developing patterns of working hard at school when we're young can be very helpful. However, if we do that exclusively, without developing friendships or participating in other activities, such as sport or music, it can be unhelpful. For Chloe, working hard at her school work was helpful, as it gave her a sense of achievement as well as forming good study patterns that she was able to resurrect when she was studying for her Leaving Cert.
Hiding her feelings of unhappiness.	Unhelpful / helpful	We've seen how hiding feelings of unhappiness can be like putting a block on a volcano, so that the person either explodes with rage, leaks out in a passive-aggressive way, or simmers with quiet distress, causing all sorts of physical or mental conditions. However, there are times when it's better for each of us to hide our feelings of unhappiness from others. This can be fine as a temporary method, so long as we know that we're doing it and we acknowledge to ourselves that we actually do feel unhappy and do something to improve things as a matter of priority.

Chloe's actions	Helpful or unhelpful?	Claire's comments
Day-dreaming.	Unhelpful	This is something many of us do and can be a pleasant way of passing the time while waiting for something. However, it was not helpful for Chloe, as it distracted her from whatever she was supposed to be doing
Recognising that she needed help when she was first cutting herself.	Helpful	This is very helpful, as it can be difficult for any of us to recognise that we could do with help. Sometimes things have to get pretty bad and we're feeling terrible before we realise that we need help. The earlier we can recognise our need for support the better.
Confiding in her guidance counsellor.	Helpful	This was extremely helpful. The death of her classmate was the catalyst for Chloe to realise that her need for help was greater than her fear of what might happen if anyone found out what she was doing. This took great courage and was a very important step in her recovery.

Chloe's actions	Helpful or unhelpful?	Claire's comments
Choosing not to move school for her last two years of secondary school.	Helpful	This was a very helpful decision for Chloe, as it meant she was standing up for herself and was not avoiding her 'difficult' classmates. However, for some pupils the decision to move to a different school and start afresh can be a helpful one too. It depends really on how able the person is to move forward without somehow seeing the move as a 'failure' and unintentionally re-creating difficulties from the previous school. The decision whether or not to move is a very individual one and depends on many things, including the personality of the person, their ability to cope and the support available.
Taking the help offered by the Child and Adolescent Mental Health Services.	Helpful	This was very obviously a helpful action for Chloe and also for her parents, who were involved in the process. There are many people who give help, there are many people who come to get help, and there are many people who take help. Chloe was one of them!
Stopping cutting herself.	Helpful	This was probably one of the most helpful actions that Chloe did. It can be very difficult to change habits, even if they're painful and self-destructive. The action of cutting can actually become an addiction, and so for Chloe to stop harming herself in this way took courage and strength of character—further proof of her ability to succeed rather than to fail.

Chloe's actions	Helpful or unhelpful?	Claire's comments
Studying hard.	Helpful	This was a very helpful action for Chloe, as it built up her confidence and meant that she was well prepared for her exams. It's important to note, though, that 'studying hard' for Chloe meant that she studied wisely. Any of us could spend hours 'studying', but if we're not focused we might just be wasting time. The benefits for pupils in learning some basic study skills that match their learning style can be enormous.
Doing well in her Leaving Cert.	Helpful	Chloe's excellent results gave her a huge boost in confidence and justified for her how hard she had worked in preparation for her exams. We might think that they would also have shattered her belief that she was stupid, not good enough and a failure. They didn't, because she attributed her success to her teachers, to the exams being easy, and to luck! It's important to emphasise that 'doing well' in exams is not a priority for everyone. We're all different, and many people who didn't do particularly well in exams live very successful lives. Equally, there are too many people who pushed themselves to achieve excellent results but who, for a range of reasons, live an unhappy life. Exam results by themselves don't lead to happiness, or to distress. It all depends on what the results mean to us, and what we do with them!

Chloe's actions	Helpful or unhelpful?	Claire's comments
Recognising that she had made the wrong choice of subject.	Helpful	The course Chloe had begun to study was different from what she had expected and was not giving her any sense of satisfaction or pleasure. Someone else might have just assumed that this was what university was like, but Chloe was astute in recognising quickly that the course simply wasn't for her. She really was like a square peg in a round hole.
Leaving university at that time.	Helpful	Chloe had described herself as 'dropping out' of university. This implies failure. I reframed her decision to leave as 'taking action to improve her life.' For Chloe this action was definitely helpful. Too many people recognise that the subject they're studying is not for them but, for whatever reason, are unable or unwilling to do anything to change things. We all know people who are clearly unhappy in the work they do but have never taken steps to do something they enjoy. That said, leaving university can for some be a very unhelpful decision: it can feed into 'I'm a failure' beliefs, and people can miss opportunities. What makes the difference really is what people do once they leave university, how they can make peace with their decision to leave, and the quality of support they avail of. Once again it's important to stress that we're all different, and going to university in the first place is not in fact helpful for everyone.

Chloe's actions	Helpful or unhelpful?	Claire's comments
Going to France, getting a job and making a success of it.	Helpful	This turned out to be a very helpful action for Chloe. It gave her many opportunities to develop her resilience in coping with changes as well as developing her language expertise. While she was slow to attribute the success of that year to herself, she did recognise that it was a success.
Returning to university to study something she wanted to do.	Helpful	It can be daunting for someone who has 'dropped out' of university to try it again. Thoughts such as *What if I make a mess of this?* and *What if I don't like this either?* can be haunting and can trigger anxiety. Many people then see the anxiety as a sign that they're not able to do whatever it is and wait until they 'feel confident.' They may wait a long time, as every time they think about whatever it is that prompts them to feel anxious they will feel anxious. It can take courage and determination to do things anyway, which is what Chloe did.

Chloe's actions	Helpful or unhelpful?	Claire's comments
Getting a first-class honours degree.	Helpful	Getting a degree is usually seen as a helpful outcome for people who have gone to university; getting a first-class honours degree can be particularly satisfying. While Chloe tended to dismiss any of her academic achievements in favour of believing that she was stupid, she found it a bit more difficult to attribute her excellent results to external factors, such as her lecturers. Deep down she did recognise that perhaps she wasn't completely stupid! Her results also justified her decision to take a year off and study something she was interested in. Her result was also helpful in her getting a place on a PhD course.
Completing her PhD.	Helpful	Some people start a PhD and then decide not to continue with it. This can be the ideal decision, as getting a PhD is not something that everyone wants to do or has to do. However, if Chloe had acted on her many thoughts, such as *I can't do this, Who am I fooling thinking that I can get a PhD?* and *I don't know why I'm bothering anyway, as I'm not good enough,* she would have left university for the second time and reinforced her own belief of being a failure.

Chloe's actions	Helpful or unhelpful?	Claire's comments
Considering a job offer when she's finished.	Helpful	Chloe didn't see this as a helpful action, as she was clear that she hadn't finished her studies yet and thought that her job offer was distracting her from them. I saw it as being very helpful, though, as it shone the spotlight on her future when she might have a job in a city she wanted to work in. As Chloe reflected on this she agreed with me and changed her initial 'Unhelpful' to 'Helpful'.
Criticising herself severely.	Unhelpful	Chloe smiled as she recognised at this stage in the process just how unhelpful this action was, and how often she did it!

Chloe's actions	Helpful or unhelpful?	Claire's comments
Developing a relationship with Mark, despite her low self-confidence and her sisters' disapproval.	Helpful	You might expect Chloe to consider this action as having been extremely unhelpful. You would be right. However, when we talked about this for a while she changed her view and decided that it was actually helpful. Her time with Mark had shattered her sense of herself as never having been able to have a relationship with a man. She had learnt a lot, and while it had been very difficult for her she had greater self-confidence now than she had before she met him. She also said she was glad that she didn't take her sisters' advice, as she 'learnt the hard way' and knew what he was really like. If she had listened to her sisters she might have spent years regretting that she hadn't followed her heart. She could see how this could hold her back from developing a strong loving relationship in the future, as she could always make comparisons with what 'might have been' with Mark. Now she knew that she was better off without him and decided with hindsight that having had the relationship was more helpful than having possibly spent years in regret or in fantasy.

Chloe's actions	Helpful or unhelpful?	Claire's comments
Walking calmly away from Mark and the other woman without saying a word to either of them.	Helpful	When Chloe replayed this in her mind she saw herself as weak and pathetic, submissively walking away, shocked and upset. The reality was that she walked away in a dignified manner. While she spent time thinking of all the things she could have screamed at both Mark and the other woman, the reality was that she didn't say anything that she now regrets. She hadn't considered that her walking away in the way she did was actually helpful for her until we spent some time looking at it and considering her options.
Continuing to torture herself for not having dealt with things differently.	Unhelpful	Chloe immediately told me that this action was unhelpful. I asked her if she would lock two young children in a dark room and leave them there without food for a week except for ten minutes each day when she would then open the door and scream abuse at them. Of course she wouldn't. She did, however, spend a lot more than ten minutes each day screaming abuse at herself for having acted instinctively in a way that seemed right to her at the time. Chloe could see that it was cruel and unfair to continue treating herself so harshly. Thinking of treating herself as if her feelings were a young child helped her to develop a sense of compassion for herself and for what she had been through.

Chloe's actions	Helpful or unhelpful?	Claire's comments
Assuming that every other woman would have known what to do.	Unhelpful	Chloe hadn't realised that this action was either 'helpful' or 'unhelpful'. For her it was just something that she did—a lot! Now when she thought about it she recognised that in fact she had no idea whether every other woman would have known what to do. She also recognised that making assumptions caused her to feel inadequate and even more of a failure, so it was easy for her to describe that action as unhelpful.
Avoiding family gatherings.	Unhelpful	Sometimes it can be helpful for us to turn down opportunities to socialise with family or friends. Examples of this might include when we're not well or when we've already made other plans that we don't want to change. In these instances it can be helpful for us not to go to the event. However, if we're avoiding them because we don't want to feel worse it can become an unhelpful action. Our anxiety or fear can grow and can become a much bigger problem. Chloe was clear that if she had gone to some family events sooner she would have received support from her parents and sisters. While she wanted to be always well and in good form when she met them, she realised that this actually put her under pressure. She had considered their help as further proof of how much of a failure she was, but now she was beginning to see how asking for and taking help are actually huge strengths.

Chloe's actions	Helpful or unhelpful?	Claire's comments
Beginning to cut herself again.	Unhelpful	Clearly cutting herself again was an unhelpful action, though it was brilliant that she recognised this so quickly and was taking steps to prevent it from becoming a more serious problem. Cutting herself as a way of feeling better was unhelpful for a number of reasons: • It hurt! • It could quickly become an addictive way of coping with any of life's challenges. • Her cutting behaviour could occur more frequently and become more severe. • There was a danger that her wounds would become infected. • She could leave permanent scars. • She lived in terror that other people would notice her scars. • It didn't actually work for long in making her feel better. • It reinforced her belief that she was a failure.
Tormenting herself because she has begun to cut herself again.	Unhelpful	At this stage in the process Chloe recognised that it was unfair of her to torment herself and could see how this only made her feel worse.

Chloe's actions	Helpful or unhelpful?	Claire's comments
Minimising the impact that Mark's actions had on her, calling it 'a stupid break-up.'	Unhelpful	Chloe hadn't realised that she had done this. When she stepped back from it she could see that her break-up was far from 'stupid'. She was actually proud that she had ended it in the way she had and realised that she had buried how upset and distressed she had been about it all.
Recognising her fear that she won't be able to stop cutting herself.	Helpful	It was important that Chloe was able to recognise that she was afraid she might not be able to stop. This meant she could concentrate on managing her fear while at the same time taking steps to change her behaviour and to stop cutting herself.
Getting help.	Helpful	Chloe told me that she had always seen 'getting help' as a sign of weakness but now realised that it was actually a strength and was a very helpful action for her.
Taking help.	Helpful	I explained the distinction between 'getting help' and 'taking help.' Chloe could immediately see that she was taking help, and she described this as helpful.

The process of examining each action and deciding whether it's helpful or unhelpful can take time. As you read down through the various actions that Chloe was doing, did you notice yourself agreeing or disagreeing with my comments? You may have noticed that some actions can be either helpful or unhelpful according to some factors, such as the context, how the person feels when they do them and what happens afterwards. Chloe was amazed to realise that she had taken many more helpful actions than she had realised. She looked at me and in a clear voice said, 'This gives me hope that you might be right and that maybe I'm not so stupid and not such a failure after all.'

The Coping Triangle process is not intended to make someone like Chloe feel better. As we've seen, her feelings made absolute sense according to what was happening to her externally as well as what she was thinking and how she was feeling. Her thoughts were all unhelpful, and she clearly believed that she was stupid, not good enough and a failure. While at first she thought that all her actions were unhelpful, she was surprised to realise that many of her actions were actually very helpful.

The third and final step in the process is the Coping Sentence. After some discussion, Chloe decided that the following six Coping Sentences were most powerful for her:

— I feel stupid because I think I could have handled things better with Mark, *but maybe I did the best I could at the time.*
— I feel embarrassed because I think that every other woman would have handled things better, *but maybe they wouldn't have.*
— I feel inadequate because I think I'm not good enough, *but I choose to recognise and appreciate what I do well.*
— I feel upset because I think I didn't handle things well, *but I choose to act in a helpful way.*
— I feel annoyed with myself because I think I've failed again, *but I choose to learn from this.*
— I feel upset because I know I want to cut myself to release tension, *but I choose to practise being kind and gentle towards myself.*

At the end of this session Chloe and I discussed how she could act in a helpful way. She decided that she would meet her sisters and tell them what had happened, thank them for their concern, and let them know that she was actually a very capable, competent woman. She also decided that she would make a few follow-up appointments with me for us to do imagery and relaxation techniques to help gently challenge her core beliefs.

The final decision Chloe made before she left for home was to treat herself to a luxurious hand cream and to use it whenever she felt the urge to cut herself.

Can you see how Chloe's belief that she was a failure kept her completely caught in a vicious circle of blaming herself for everything? She was never going to see herself as a success or as succeeding in any way as long as she was driven by this powerful belief. Interestingly, some people have a deep belief that they're not good enough and don't deserve success and so can sabotage it. They may also develop a fear of success, which means that they live their lives as 'failures' in their own eyes. Once they become aware that this is only a belief and that perhaps it's all right for them to succeed, wonderful changes can happen.

Success can be difficult, though. Think of Elvis Presley. He was an ordinary person with a fabulous voice who was catapulted into fame. In a very short time he had become addicted to substances to help him cope, withdrew into apparent isolation and died young. We could begin writing a list of 'celebrities' we 'know' who have done the same. It would be a long list. I've deliberately put the word 'know' in quotation marks: one of the consequences of social media is that someone who becomes a success immediately becomes public property.

The pressures facing someone who succeeds in the twenty-first century are increasing at an extraordinary rate. We live in an age when some children want to be a 'celebrity' when they grow up. They watch television programmes that show that the dream of being discovered, recognised, appreciated and possibly adored is possible. They see people who constantly look happy and who seem to have no financial pressures. They obviously 'have it all,' and they can become role models for everyone else who wants to have it all too.

There's a saying, 'Please don't put me on a pedestal,' because there's a long way to fall. Some people spend their lives trying to climb onto a pedestal; others win a competition or are discovered and are immediately elevated to fame. There are others who actually don't want to be on any sort of pedestal. These are people who have worked hard and who have achieved recognition and success as a result of their own efforts. Interestingly, there are millions of such people around the world whose lives have influenced ours for the better, but we don't know them by name. We don't know what they like to wear, where they like to shop or what music they like to listen to. Their identity is not tied up with being known or famous, and they wear their success lightly.

What happens to those people who, for whatever reason, land on the pedestal of success? Some jump willingly off as soon as they can, as they find the price far too high. Others devote themselves with steely determination to remain there. Some find themselves thrown off and may spend the rest of their lives seeing themselves as failures or decide to devote themselves to climbing back up.

What are we all doing? Why is it that people who work hard and who contribute something to the world can be glorified and idolised, or hated and ridiculed? Too many actors, musicians, writers, athletes and politicians have found not just that their privacy is compromised but that they no longer have any privacy at all. A film that has had a great influence on me is

The Truman Show. This is about a television station that buys a newborn baby and streams his every waking moment to millions of viewers. As he gets older and becomes an adult he doesn't realise that everyone else in his life is actually an actor. Sadly, this story is not entirely fiction any more, as some families willingly allow almost every moment of their lives to be viewed by a voyeuristic public who want more and more sensationalism. One of the crucial moments in *The Truman Show* is when the show ends suddenly. Irritated viewers bang their televisions for a few moments but then switch channels to become absorbed in something else.

If we're not careful, success can become as addictive as a drug. People may not realise how easily they can become dependent on other people's approval to make them 'feel good.' They may experience difficult withdrawal symptoms, such as thinking that they're not good enough and will never be good enough again. We wouldn't be surprised then if they feel frightened, anxious, panicky, worried and deeply distressed. They might believe that they're actually not good enough, or they might believe that they need other people's approval to feel good about themselves.

People can respond to their thoughts, feelings and beliefs in a range of ways. They can actively seek out something that will give them the 'buzz' of success once more, not realising that they need a greater volume of approval. And they can do the opposite: they can decide that no matter how hard they work they're never going to achieve the level of success they first had and give up.

Tragically, some people choose to take their own life, while others, in the words of Henry David Thoreau, 'lead lives of quiet desperation.'

Exercise 11.1 is designed to give you a few moments to reflect on how this chapter has affected you.

Exercise 11.1: *Failure and success exercise*

Complete the following sentences:

1. Failure and success are

2. The thing that struck me most in reading this chapter is

3. Having read this I now choose to

If we live our lives so as to be seen by other people as a 'success', maybe we're not actually succeeding in living our own lives.

My final question for you before we move on to the next chapter is: Would you consider it a success to acknowledge moments of 'failure', to learn from them and to keep going anyway? I would, and I do. My favourite ending to the Coping Sentence is *but I choose to learn from this.*

Chapter 12
Change

The only thing that is constant is change.

—HERACLITUS

*I knew who I was this morning, but I've changed
a few times since then.*

—LEWIS CARROLL

C hange is inevitable, but it can leave us feeling very uncertain about who we are and what's going on for us. Any of us who have experienced huge change suddenly and unexpectedly will know how our lives can be defined by it. Suddenly there is a life that was 'before' and a life that was 'after'. This is not necessarily a bad thing, but we often assume that it is.

Change can creep up unnoticed until suddenly we look in the mirror and wonder where those 'laughter lines' have suddenly come from! Some changes can be anticipated with fear and dread. Thoughts of important moments of change, such as a child's first day in school, a young adult leaving home or an older person retiring, can be enough to trigger acute feelings of distress, upset, panic and fear. While change can definitely be difficult, it is not always so. Also, while we may not like change, one of our most useful characteristics as human beings is our ability to adapt. Sometimes we can surprise ourselves, as well as others, by how quickly we cope with changes when they arrive.

One of the core tenets of Buddhist teaching is that suffering is part of life. By accepting that any change can bring with it some level of distress we give ourselves space for looking at how we can cope with it as well as we can. The reality of change can be hugely comforting, as it can give us a sense of hope that 'this too will pass.' The *idea* of change can be terrifying, however, and many of us anticipate change with fear and dread. Deep down we all know that, whatever actually happens to change our circumstances, we have two real choices: either we cope or we don't. If we can learn to welcome change into our lives we will increase our ability to cope with it.

The internet is a great source of 'information' that seems accurate but often needs to be verified. Apparently the 'fact' that the Bible contains the phrase 'do not fear' a total of 365 times is not true: the correct number seems to vary, but the consensus is that readers of the Bible are advised many times not to fear. That supports my view that 'reassurance doesn't work'! It doesn't because deep down we don't believe that it's all right not to fear. No-one can really tell us that whatever we're afraid might happen will not happen. It just may. No-one can really convince us that the worst—whatever that is—will not happen, as it may. Thinking this way can be very difficult, as it can trigger a range of intense, distressing feelings, including, at times, hopelessness. So how can the Welcoming Approach help us to cope with change?

ERIC

Eric's story is a good example of how some people have learnt to cope successfully with change. He is not real, but the issues I describe are.

Eric first came to see me when he was fifty-nine. He was recommended to do so by his personnel manager, who recognised that he seemed to have difficulty in adjusting to changes within the company. He was at first very guarded with me and questioned me as to whether I was going to 'diagnose him as incompetent.'

Eric explained that he had begun work with the company when he left school, had worked as a senior manager for the previous fifteen years and had fully expected to be there for another six years, until he retired. The company had undergone radical restructuring in the previous eight months, and a number of his colleagues had been offered redundancy packages. Eric looked straight at me and said, 'I was offered redundancy three times, and three times I said no. I like my work, and I don't want you or anyone else forcing me to leave a day before I have to, when I'm sixty-five years old.'

It was clear that Eric saw himself as having been 'sent' to me. He explained that he was 'doing what he was told' but that he didn't 'need' to be with me. He had only followed the recommendation to come and see me as he thought that if he didn't it could somehow come against him and he could be described as being 'obstructive'.

Eric asked me how I worked and how I thought I could 'help' him, when he clearly didn't need and didn't want help. We had a very interesting thirty-minute conversation, during which I had an opportunity to give Eric a brief overview of how I worked. He said that he liked my emphasis on working together collaboratively to develop coping skills, but as he was coping really well anyway he didn't want to waste his time, or mine. We agreed not to continue with the session and said goodbye, holding each other in mutual regard.

Two years later Eric made another appointment with me. The man I met in the waiting-room contrasted sharply with the one I had met previously. He looked tired, drained and deeply unhappy. The energy and certainty that had been so much a part of him seemed to have disappeared. When Eric entered my office he took a moment to look round and stared at the chair he had sat in before. He turned to look at me with sadness and distress in his expression and his voice. 'I didn't think that I'd ever see you again,' he told me in a quiet voice. 'I'm so embarrassed at how arrogant I was when I met you before. I don't think you could have helped me then, because I didn't see any need for you to do so, but I hope and pray that you can help me now.'

His voice broke a little with emotion as he explained that since we had met he had experienced huge changes in his life. His employer had insisted that he take early retirement. His wife, Marie, had been told she had cancer, and two of his three children had emigrated to live thousands of miles away. He no longer had any contact with his colleagues and realised that, even though he had considered them his closest friends, they were actually not.

I asked Eric to choose something that was particularly distressing for him so that we could work together to see how the Welcoming Approach could help him. He looked at me and very earnestly said, 'My whole life.' Fig. 12.1 shows Eric's thoughts, feelings and actions as he did step 1 of the Coping Triangle.

What do you think it was like for Eric to do this first step? When I asked him this he shrugged and said, 'If I had taken your help two years ago I might not be here now.' I asked him how he felt when he thought that. He was silent for a moment and then said, 'Frustrated and angry with myself.' My sense was that he was blaming himself for whatever was going on in his life, and I wondered if he saw the fact that he had come back to me as proof of 'failure'. He nodded in agreement.

Eric told me that he didn't really think I was going to help him, as I couldn't change what had happened to him or his wife and I couldn't prevent the awful changes that were going to happen in the future. I agreed with him. He looked at me a little surprised and said, 'Well, if you can't help me, why am I here?'

This led to an interesting conversation in which we explored the fact that if Eric believed that coming to see me was further

Fig. 12.1: Step 1 of Eric's Coping Triangle

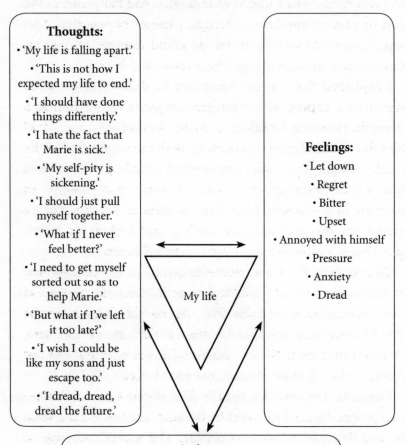

Thoughts:
- 'My life is falling apart.'
- 'This is not how I expected my life to end.'
- 'I should have done things differently.'
- 'I hate the fact that Marie is sick.'
- 'My self-pity is sickening.'
- 'I should just pull myself together.'
- 'What if I never feel better?'
- 'I need to get myself sorted out so as to help Marie.'
- 'But what if I've left it too late?'
- 'I wish I could be like my sons and just escape too.'
- 'I dread, dread, dread the future.'

My life

Feelings:
- Let down
- Regret
- Bitter
- Upset
- Annoyed with himself
- Pressure
- Anxiety
- Dread

Actions:
- Torture myself with pictures of how my life 'should be.'
- Blame myself.
- Hide my feelings from everyone.
- Worry.
- Wish I had done things differently.
- Watch 'films' of my life getting worse and worse.
- Resort to asking for help.

proof of how terrible his life was, he was going to be right. He was also right that I couldn't change what had happened in the past or prevent any future changes. I knew, though, that if he was prepared to work with me we could together change his own attitude towards his past, his present and his future.

I explained that I saw the fact that he decided to get some support for coping with whatever was going on for him as a strength. However, I couldn't convince him of this, and I told him that if he believed that working with me wouldn't work he would be right. You'll understand why I added: 'But maybe this is an opportunity for you to look at whatever is going on in your life in a new way. Maybe the process of standing back a little from how awful you're feeling, and looking at what's going on in a different way, might make a difference.'

Eric thought for a few moments quietly to himself. We had gone past the point at which he had ended the previous session two years earlier, and he was obviously considering whether he should leave this one too. He then looked at me and said, 'Maybe you're right. There's no point in being here if I'm not going to give it a chance; so tell me what I need to do.'

I explained that we had already done the first step of a three-step process by catching what he thought, how he felt and what he was doing in relation to his life. The second step was to consider four questions. Eric looked surprised when I asked him the first of these: Did his feelings make sense? 'Of course they don't make sense,' he replied a little snappily. 'I've worked hard all my life. I fully expected to stay in my job until I was sixty-five, and to leave with a good pension and to enjoy the time I had left with my wife. Why would it make sense for me to feel as terrible as I do?'

Do you see Eric's feelings as making sense? I do. I say this on the grounds that he was obviously experiencing life itself as a challenge and also on the grounds of what he was thinking and what he was doing. Eric expected himself to feel happy. He judged himself harshly because he felt increasingly unhappy. He decided that this was all his fault, because he was doing something wrong.

Eric was at the stage of his life when he had thought things would get easier for him; instead his wife was seriously ill and his two older children had emigrated. He spent time reflecting on how his present situation was completely his fault and dreading the future. Given all this, how could he really expect to feel good?

Eric recognised quite quickly that each of his thoughts was unhelpful. This only seemed to make him feel worse, and I was very aware that he was finding it difficult to stay and not to give up on the session. He listened carefully to my explanation of core beliefs, and we worked together to see if we could identify any particular beliefs he had that might have been causing him particular distress.

One of his principal thoughts was 'I should have done things differently.' He agreed to work with me to tease out the meaning behind this thought and to see if we could uncover a core belief. Fig. 12.2 shows the process Eric went through in doing this.

Eric looked sadly at me. 'It's true. I'm not supposed to fail. I've spent my whole life working hard to succeed, and now, just when it's my time to enjoy my life, I've messed it all up.'

He described leaving the job he had enjoyed in very difficult circumstances. He had refused to take the redundancy package that had been offered two years before, preferring to keep working with the company until he reached the retirement age of sixty-five. He hadn't realised that this wasn't an option, as the company's restructuring meant that the role he had in it no longer existed. If he was to continue working with the company he needed to be adaptable, to retrain and to move somewhere else. Eric fought against these changes but lost. After a bitter battle that involved solicitors, he agreed to accept the redundancy.

Fig. 12.2: Eric's process in uncovering one of his core beliefs

	I should have done things differently.
What's so bad about not having done things differently?	↓
	I've let people down.
What's so bad about having let people down?	↓
	They won't like it and will be annoyed with me.
What's so bad about people not liking it and their being annoyed with you?	↓
	I haven't done enough.
What's so bad about not having done enough?	↓
	I've failed.
What's so bad about having failed?	↓
	I'm not supposed to fail.

Now, six months later, he was tortured by the thought that he had done the wrong thing. He saw leaving the company as one of the biggest mistakes he could have made and spent time wishing that he had been able to adapt to the changes.

When I asked him why he thought he hadn't been able to do this he said, with absolute certainty, 'Because I'm no good with change.'

I asked Eric what age he thought he was when he first began to believe this. He didn't know; as far back as he could remember he had hated all kinds of change. He found the transition from primary school to secondary school very difficult. When he left school he began a training scheme with his company and remained there his entire working life. He pitied people who didn't seem settled and who always seemed to be looking for something else, and he described his liking things being the way they were as a good thing.

When he met his future wife she quickly learnt that he didn't like change. They kept their first car until it was declared dangerous, then bought another one of the same make and the same colour. Eric laughed as he said, 'Actually, I still drive that make of car, and have never changed to one of a different colour!'

There were many examples of how he had resisted change. He and his family went to the same place on holiday, and at the same time, every year. His dislike of change even influenced the type of shoes he wore year after year. He agreed to do the Downward Arrow technique again to see if we could work out what was behind his dislike of change. This process is shown in fig. 12.3.

Fig. 12.3: Eric's process in uncovering his core belief about change

	I don't like change.
What's so bad about change?	↓
	Change is never good.

He stopped at this point and looked at me with surprise. 'My grandmother used to say that all the time I was young,' he told me. He hadn't realised that he had been influenced at a very young age by his grandmother's dislike of change. I asked him to list three examples that would prove that change is never good. He energetically took to this task; his replies are shown in table 12.1.

Table 12.1: Eric's 'proof that change is never good'

Redundancy	Life is boring, isolating, and financially poorer.
Health	Changes in health cause pain, worry, and sooner or later death.
Children growing up	They move away to a different country, and life is never the same again.

Eric looked up at me as he was writing and asked me if he was supposed to feel better doing this exercise, as he definitely did not. He smiled as I asked him if his feelings made sense, and he nodded that they did. He told me that as he was writing his list he was thinking of how good life was before all these changes and how terrible it is now—so, yes, it made sense that he wasn't feeling great as he wrote.

He agreed to do a second exercise on change, which was to list three proofs that some changes are good. His replies are shown in table 12.2.

Table 12.2: Eric's list of 'some changes that are good'

Clean clothes	Important for hygiene.
Books to read	It can be boring to read the same book over and over again.
Football teams playing different teams in different places	They improve as they get variety.
Elections	Politicians can't get too complacent and need to be responsible if they want to be re-elected.

As you can see, Eric gave four proofs instead of three. He seemed a bit bewildered and said, 'I never considered that change could actually be good, but I see that it is really essential.' He was clear, though, that there was nothing good in the changes he was struggling to cope with.

I suggested that perhaps there was something good in his being made redundant. Maybe there was something good in the fact that his wife was told she had cancer, and maybe there was something good in his two older children emigrating.

He looked away for a few moments and then said, 'I really do hate being wrong!' He then laughed and said, 'You know, you're right.' Now that he gave himself permission to change focus and look at these three challenges from a different viewpoint he could see that having been made redundant meant that he now had more time to support his wife and for them to do things together. While the diagnosis of her cancer was frightening, it meant that she could get treatment. He wasn't sure how his children living thousands of miles away could be a good change, but then he laughed aloud as he said, 'I'm getting great practice at using Skype!'

Now that Eric was gently challenging his own belief about change I decided to talk to him about the change that awaits each one of us: death. We looked at how his life had changed following the death of people he loved. His maternal grandmother had died when he was seven, and he described clearly remembering the light having gone out of his mother's face. He reflected more to himself: 'I'm not sure if it was ever fully turned on again.' Eric's father died when he was seventeen and his mother when he was forty-two. The death of his parents had been very difficult for him, and he told me that he dreaded dying and so causing his own children similar heartbreak.

As we talked about this a little more, however, Eric realised that somehow, without actually realising it, he had coped with the death of the three people he loved most as a child and as a young man. He softly said, 'So I'll cope too if Marie dies before I do.' He said it again with conviction, and then added, 'And my children will cope too.'

At this point Eric looked straight at me once more and said, 'I'm relieved that I've realised that some changes are good. This gives me hope and makes me wonder if maybe I haven't failed in everything I've done either!' He had realised that just because he believed whatever he believed, for as long as he had believed it, it didn't make his beliefs true. This realisation gave him a welcome sense of hope.

It's easy to see how a lot of Eric's actions in his Coping Triangle were unhelpful. The one that was probably most unhelpful was how cruel he was at times in judging himself a failure. As we worked together it was obvious that he automatically did many helpful actions. For instance, he listened to new ideas and reflected carefully on them. He willingly and courageously questioned beliefs that he had held for a long time.

Perhaps his action that I considered to be most helpful was his willingness to embrace change. Once he questioned his belief that all change was bad, and that things that had affected his life were always his fault, he decided to take immediate steps to change things. He became animated as he wondered aloud if his wife was well enough to take a trip abroad to visit each of their children.

He had jumped towards the Coping Sentence before I had even explained it. Not surprisingly, when we moved to the third step of the Coping Sentence the one he liked best was:

I feel disappointed / annoyed / sad because I think I have allowed my fear of change to limit my life, *but I'm now ready to embrace change.*

Eric understood that embracing change could cause him to feel distressed and anxious, just as chemotherapy could make Marie feel sick and frightened. He had heard of Susan Jeffers's book *Feel the Fear and Do It Anyway* and decided to act on my suggestion that he 'feel the fear and do it anyway with understanding and self-compassion.'

Eric left my office a little clearer in his understanding of why he reacted so rigidly to change. He understood that he would have moments, many moments, in his life when he would feel distressed, particularly when he was challenged by change. He had changed, though, from the man I had met before the session. He was no longer prepared to automatically blame himself for every challenging thing that happened in his life. He decided to deliberately challenge himself to create changes in his life, and to make a follow-up appointment with me in a few weeks to review how he had got on and to obtain further support, if appropriate.

This chapter began with two quotations about two features of change: it's constant, and it can leave us not knowing who we are or what is happening. I'm going to finish it with two other powerful quotations.

> *It is not the strongest of the species that survive, nor the most intelligent, but the one most responsive to change.*
>
> CHARLES DARWIN

> *The curious paradox is that when I accept myself just as I am, then I can change.*
>
> CARL ROGERS

Chapter 13
Conclusion

The end is in the beginning and yet you go on.

—SAMUEL BECKETT

What do you think of the Welcoming Approach? Sometimes it's easy to welcome people, experiences or opportunities; sometimes it's not. Imagine you're at home and your front doorbell rings. As you go to answer it you see all the objects that are not supposed to be in your hall. You realise that you've no time to tidy up. You open the door to see standing there someone you love, and you breathe a sigh of relief. You know that they won't judge you by the state of your home, and you welcome them in.

Would you have the same sense of relief if the person at your door was someone you thought of as being critical of you? You might immediately begin to apologise or to blame yourself for not having had your home tidy enough for visitors.

Sometimes it's easy to welcome feelings of distress; sometimes it's not. If we judge our feelings as making sense it can free us a little from being so self-critical and judgemental. The Welcoming Approach is a way of gently doing this in a very logical, systematic way. It doesn't mean that we won't feel distressed. As you've seen, sometimes we might actually feel more distressed as we courageously face whatever it is that's causing us upset. It's not enough to do the first step of the Coping Triangle and catch whatever we're thinking, feeling and doing in relation to something that's upsetting us.

The four questions in step 2 are logical. Do our feelings make sense? In my experience they always do, according to whatever is going on in our lives and/or what we're thinking and what we're doing.

Are our thoughts helpful or unhelpful? Please don't worry if you notice yourself having lots and lots of unhelpful thoughts. Instead welcome the fact that you're recognising that they're unhelpful, which immediately reduces their power to harm you. How about beginning to see your thoughts as people ringing your doorbell? Some will be wonderful and some might be extremely critical. Once you recognise thoughts as being 'unhelpful' you reduce their power to torture you.

The third question, 'What do you believe?' is crucial. Sometimes it can be important to uncover exactly which belief is driving us to think, feel and act in a certain way. Often, though, it can be enough to know that we could believe something that may not be true. Questioning our beliefs can open our eyes to seeing things that disprove these, as we saw with Eric in the last chapter.

The reason the Coping Triangle is designed in the shape of a downward triangle is to place emphasis on actions. The fourth question in step 2 is 'Are your actions helpful or unhelpful?' It can be very easy to think of all the actions we do that are unhelpful; it's very important to consider the actions we do that are helpful. Sometimes it's easier to do this if we see ourselves as young children coming to an adult with a drawing we've just done. The picture we drew might not be perfect: we might not have used the right colours, or we might even have made a terrible mess. Most adults, though, would instinctively concentrate on what the child had done well. We all do things well too!

The third step of the Coping Triangle is essential. The Coping Sentence provides a clear framework for acknowledging our feelings, for linking them to something that makes sense and concentrating on helpful action we choose to take.

Throughout this book we've looked at how people with a range of concerns have used the Welcoming Approach. You may have related to one or two of these in particular, and you may have noticed yourself feeling irritated, bored or uninterested while reading some others. You may even have noticed yourself switching off. I encourage you to welcome your feelings, whatever they are. Become aware of what you're thinking, question your beliefs, and concentrate on what you choose to do to respond proactively. Sometimes we can actually do this better when we're not feeling great. So, regardless of how you feel right now, if it makes sense that's all right. But what are you going to do about it?

Do you remember Anna and Richard? Anna is the little girl at the start of this book who was upset because her balloon flew away. How would our world be if three-year-old children automatically knew to say:

> I feel upset, sad and cross because my balloon blew away, *but that's all right.*

It is all right to feel upset, sad and cross when we lose something that we value.

Richard is Anna's friend who had a difficult childhood and grew up to have a difficult life. How would his life have been if he was able to say:

> I feel frightened and confused because my parents are fighting, and I think it's my fault, *but maybe it's not.*

It's never too late to begin to allow ourselves to feel our feelings of distress, upset, anger, hurt, regret, guilt, loneliness or depression. We can all learn to recognise thoughts as 'helpful' or 'unhelpful' and to challenge what we learnt to believe without question many years ago. The best news is that we can always, always learn to act in a helpful way, to treat ourselves with kindness and compassion, to learn to recognise and to appreciate what we do well, and what others do well, and to learn to forgive and to let go.

Life can be demanding enough without us causing ourselves greater upset because we 'don't feel happy.' Interestingly, though, it can often be more difficult for us to welcome things that are going really well for us. How often have you heard people say that they're afraid to celebrate their good fortune, as they fear that it won't last and they'll feel worse after feeling good? It seems a bit odd, really! Let's welcome all our feelings of distress, all our thoughts and beliefs about all life's challenges, and focus on transforming these in a way that is helpful for us.

Let's practise coping and let's follow Rumi's advice and live a life of welcoming!

COPYRIGHT PERMISSIONS